Everything Is Police

Forerunners: Ideas First

Short books of thought-in-process scholarship, where intense analysis, questioning, and speculation take the lead

FROM THE UNIVERSITY OF MINNESOTA PRESS

Mick Smith and Jason Young
Does the Earth Care? Indifference, Providence, and Provisional Ecology

Caterina Albano
Out of Breath: Vulnerability of Air in Contemporary Art

Gregg Lambert
The World Is Gone: Philosophy in Light of the Pandemic

Grant Farred
Only a Black Athlete Can Save Us Now

Anna Watkins Fisher
Safety Orange

Heather Warren-Crow and Andrea Jonsson
Young-Girls in Echoland: #Theorizing Tiqqun

Joshua Schuster and Derek Woods
Calamity Theory: Three Critiques of Existential Risk

Daniel Bertrand Monk and Andrew Herscher
The Global Shelter Imaginary: IKEA Humanitarianism and Rightless Relief

Catherine Liu
Virtue Hoarders: The Case against the Professional Managerial Class

Christopher Schaberg
Grounded: Perpetual Flight . . . and Then the Pandemic

Marquis Bey
The Problem of the Negro as a Problem for Gender

Cristina Beltrán
Cruelty as Citizenship: How Migrant Suffering Sustains White Democracy

Hil Malatino
Trans Care

Sarah Juliet Lauro
Kill the Overseer! The Gamification of Slave Resistance

Alexis L. Boylan, Anna Mae Duane, Michael Gill, and Barbara Gurr
Furious Feminisms: Alternate Routes on *Mad Max: Fury Road*

Ian G. R. Shaw and Marv Waterstone
Wageless Life: A Manifesto for a Future beyond Capitalism

(Continued on page 100)

Everything Is Police

Tia Trafford

University of Minnesota Press
MINNEAPOLIS
LONDON

Portions of chapter 1 were previously published in "The World as Police," *Rhizomes: Cultural Studies in Emerging Knowledge,* no. 38 (2022).

ISBN 978-1-5179-1686-2 (PB)
ISBN 978-1-4529-7079-0 (Ebook)
ISBN 978-1-4529-7160-5 (Manifold)

Published by the University of Minnesota Press, 2024
111 Third Avenue South, Suite 290
Minneapolis, MN 55401-2520
www.upress.umn.edu

Available as a Manifold edition at manifold.umn.edu

The University of Minnesota is an equal-opportunity educator and employer.

Contents

Introduction: Lynching from the Days of Slavery

> Deaths at the hands of police and other state actors and substate actors are so frequent and so numerous as to be a normal part of Black life.
>
> —RINALDO WALCOTT

WHY DO WE NEED POLICE? Why do we police one another? Why feel this pull, this desire to police and to be policed?

Stephen Lawrence was eighteen when he was stabbed to death by a group of white racists in Southeast London. His best friend, Duwayne Brooks, later described his murder as "like a lynching from the days of slavery." Speaking amid Britain's Home Office hostilities and institutionalized anti-Blackness, Doreen Lawrence also located her son Stephen's killing within what Derek Gregory terms the "colonial present":

> [The police] treated the affair as a gang war and from that moment on acted in a manner that can only be described as white masters during slavery. . . . Everything in this country has Black people who have played a part in it. . . . We helped to make the National Health Service what it is today, we have good transport, you name it and we have been a part of it. . . . My feelings about the future remain the same as they were when my son was murdered. Black youngsters will never be safe on the streets. . . . The police on the ground are the same as they were when my son was killed. I am hearing killing on the streets and in the back of police vans and it is clear that nothing has changed.

1

Considering the content of this statement and Doreen Lawrence's invocation that "nothing has changed," I want to read the phrase "future remain the same" as not only an expression of feeling. I read "future remain the same" as also expressing the colonial present by situating anti-Black violence across the reverberating spatio-temporalities of colonial modernity. The colonial present denotes more than how trajectories of slavery, colonialism, and imperialism continue into the present. The colonial present also suggests how colonial modernity shifted to accommodate formal equality while leaving its frameworks unexamined and the plantation system reorganized rather than ended.[1] That "future remain the same" does not collapse histories into analogy, nor does it suggest that history is static. Rather, the death of Stephen Lawrence is articulated as a multifaceted moment *within* transatlantic slavery, plantation, apartheid, segregation, colonization, dependency of the Global North on the labor of peripheral nations, the police van.

It has been central to abolitionist thought and praxis to articulate policing and incarceration as infrastructures for anti-Black violence within the colonial present. Foregrounding the circulations of police and control that reverberated across colony and metropole also centers how policing has been a constant variable in violence perpetuated in white capitalist society.[2]

1. Saidiya Hartman, *Scenes of Subjection: Terror, Slavery, and Self-Making in Nineteenth-Century America* (New York: Oxford University Press, 2010), 119; Christina Sharpe, *In the Wake: On Blackness and Being* (Durham, N.C.: Duke University Press, 2016), 73.

2. E.g., Biko Agozino, *Counter-colonial Criminology: A Critique of Imperialist Reason* (London: Pluto Press, 2003); Michelle Alexander, *The New Jim Crow: Mass Incarceration in the Age of Colorblindness* (New York: New Press, 2012); Mike Brodgen, "The Emergence of the Police—the Colonial Dimension," *British Journal of Criminology* 27, no. 1 (1987): 4–14; Mark Brown, *Penal Power and Colonial Rule* (Abingdon, U.K.: Routledge, 2014); Partha Chatterjee, *The Black Hole of Empire: History of a Global Practice of Power* (Princeton, N.J.: Princeton University Press, 2012);

For example, on Barbados, slave resistance was considered as both pervasive atmosphere of potential disorder and contingent eruption of rebellion.[3] There slave codes and patrols set up structures that were later translated across what became the United States, empire, plantation, and colony. The codes both justified and wrote Blackness into law, while also signifying the existence of early forms of institutionalized police in slave pass check searches, patrols, and targeting.[4]

These connections have long been drawn by abolitionist writers, who consider the origins of the police as invested in racial hierarchy, punishment, and exploitation. They are vital to understanding how policing employs colonial counterinsurgency (COIN) strategies that

---

Bankole A. Cole, "Post-colonial Systems," in *Policing across the World: Issues for the Twenty-First Century,* ed. R. I. Mawby, 88–108 (London: UCL Press, 1999); J. M. Moore, "Is the Empire Coming Home? Liberalism, Exclusion and the Punitiveness of the British State," *Papers from the British Criminology Conference* 14 (2014): 31–48; Dylan Rodríguez, "Tyranny of the Task Force: Police Abolition and the Counterinsurgent Campus," *Connecticut Law Review* 506 (2021); Stuart Schrader, *Badges without Borders: How Global Counterinsurgency Transformed American Policing* (Oakland: University of California Press, 2019); Georgina Sinclair, *At the End of the Line: Colonial Policing and the Imperial Endgame 1945–80* (Manchester, U.K.: Manchester University Press, 2006).

3. Following Saidiya Hartman (and many of the writers discussed later), I tend to use *slave* rather than *enslaved person*—as a term that encapsulates the position and logics of subjection. Hartman, *Scenes.* Where necessary, I also leave intact quotations containing words that are now considered slurs, both for historical accuracy and to ensure that the conceptual distinctions in their use are not blurred.

4. E.g., Douglas Blackmon, *Slavery by Another Name: The Reenslavement of Black Americans from the Civil War to World War II* (New York: Doubleday, 2008); Angela Davis, "From the Prison of Slavery to the Slavery of Prison: Frederick Douglass and the Convict Lease System," in *The Angela Y. Davis Reader,* ed. Joy James, 74–95 (Malden, Mass.: Blackwell, 1998); Sally Hadden, *Slave Patrols: Law and Violence in Virginia and the Carolinas* (Cambridge, Mass.: Harvard University Press, 2001); Sarah Haley, *No Mercy Here: Gender, Punishment and the Making of Jim Crow Modernity* (Chapel Hill: University of North Carolina Press, 2016); Marcus Rediker, *The Slave Ship: A Human History* (New York: Penguin, 2007).

envelop the polity within the operations of a domestic "colonizing army," as Salmon Rushdie wrote of 1980s Britain. These trajectories of thought consider how police exist to protect and produce systems of exploitation and inequality.[5]

What follows in this book attempts to push further through these accounts that situate policing in the context of slave patrol and colonial counterinsurgency. Reverberating across the colonial present, and practically universally, as Frank B. Wilderson III identifies, Black people are policed all the time and everywhere. But as such, articulating the universality of policing moves beyond police exceptionalism.[6] I want to think about how policing was embedded into the structures of white society, with the armed police force its overt manifestation. This is to concentrate less on its institutionalization and more on how the world itself came to be shaped in the image of police.

I will suggest that across colonial modernity, police emerged as a world-shaping force as well as the form of both civil society and the world under creation. As Sylvia Wynter teaches, the European understanding of the world ruptured and coalesced amid the globalizing traces of Columbus's landing in the Caribbean in 1492. Modernity's imaginary trailed and consolidated in the wake of the European expansionist project.[7] The radical breach of the Middle Passage was an epochal trans-formation inaugurated on a global

---

5. See Mark Neocleous, *The Fabrication of Social Order: A Critical Theory of Police Power* (London: Pluto Press, 2000); Nikhil Pal Singh, "The Whiteness of Police," *American Quarterly* 66, no. 4 (2014): 1092; Alex Vitale, *The End of Policing* (London: Verso Books, 2017), 32.

6. This follows and expands on Wilderson's thought that "white people are not simply 'protected' by the police, they are—in their very corporeality—the police." Frank B. Wilderson III, "The Prison Slave as Hegemony's (Silent) Scandal," *Social Justice* 30. no. 2 (2003): 18–27.

7. Rinaldo Walcott, *The Long Emancipation: Moving toward Black Freedom* (Durham, N.C.: Duke University Press, 2021).

scale.[8] Across the attempted installation of a Manichean infrastructure, as Frantz Fanon describes, this led to struggles to create a world through this breach of order and disorder, slave and master, colonizer and colonized, law and nature. Transatlantic slavery, Rinaldo Walcott writes, was a route "for the invention of blackness; death—the central motif of Black life, its birth through death."[9]

Reaching toward the reorganization of the earth as "world," the tendrils of the breach were woven from the expulsion of the Moors from Iberia, early enslavement of Black Africans by the Portuguese, plantations on São Tomé worked by Congolese slaves.[10] Through the vehement conscription of non-Europeans into the project of modernity, discontinuity and partition were shaped in the force of genocide, destruction of religion and culture, deracination, concentration, working people to death.[11] The breach was inaugurated by a material and sociopolitical barrage of practices that make Black people legible to Europeans as a "source of their own renewal and future possibilities."[12] As Tyrone Palmer suggests,

> the World here names an ensemble of processes that function to ensure Europe's domination of the globe and the genocidal mode of its expansion. It also names a space of enclosure and violently imposed order.[13]

The glistening utopia of Enlightenment has been a shivering carapace of retraction and deceit—a world sutured under terror and brute violence.

8. Hartman, *Scenes,* 72; Jared Sexton, "Unbearable Blackness," *Cultural Critique* 90 (2015): 166.

9. Walcott, *Long,* 15.

10. José Buscaglia-Salgado, *Undoing Empire: Race and Nation in the Mulatto Caribbean* (Minneapolis: University of Minnesota Press, 2003).

11. Lindon Barrett, *Racial Blackness and the Discontinuity of Western Modernity* (Champaign: University of Illinois Press, 2013); David Scott, *Conscripts of Modernity: The Tragedy of Colonial Enlightenment* (Durham, N.C.: Duke University Press, 2004).

12. Walcott, *Long,* 19.

13. Tyrone S. Palmer, "Otherwise Than Blackness: Feeling, World, Sublimation," *Qui Parle: Critical Humanities and Social Sciences* 29, no. 2 (2020): 253.

The breach troubles the way attention is often drawn to unilateral conquest and frontier, with "savage" and "civilizer" supposedly bound together at Europe's expanding edges. It is often said that the modern world was built on a contradiction between emancipation and democracy, on one hand, and enslavement and genocide, on the other.[14] The idea is that the violent excesses of the modern world are either an anomaly or indicate the unequal application of otherwise universal achievements in reason, freedom, and law. On this picture, a violent boundary is imposed at the frontier of civilization to maintain and produce the security of civil order.[15]

Police are written as a thin blue line in the contemporary rewriting of this story: of ever-present crises of potential societal disintegration (knife crime, drugs, gangs, migrants). The underlying myth is that police are required to uphold bourgeois civilization against possible regression. Police supposedly operate at the frontier, where the security of civil order begins to dissipate and relies on violence rather than hegemony.[16]

The picture relies on a characterization of colonialism as irrational or libidinal excess that can be reduced to violence at the boundaries of an otherwise civil order.[17] This is why Enlightenment—as it became known—is seen to contain this contradictory pull toward freedom, on one hand, and enslavement, on the other. This antinomy

14. This is practically endemic to liberal political philosophy, but see, e.g., Barnor Hesse, "Racialized Modernity: An Analytics of White Mythologies," *Ethnic and Racial Studies* 30, no. 4 (2007): 643–63; Charles W. Mills, "The Chronopolitics of Racial Time," *Time and Society* 29, no. 2 (2020): 297–317; Walter Mignolo, *The Darker Side of Western Modernity: Global Futures, Decolonial Options* (Durham, N.C.: Duke University Press, 2011); Iris Marion Young, *Justice and the Politics of Difference* (Princeton, N.J.: Princeton University Press, 2011).

15. Tyler Wall, "The Police Invention of Humanity: Notes on the 'Thin Blue Line,'" *Crime, Media, Culture* 16, no. 3 (2020): 319–36.

16. Frank B. Wilderson III, "Gramsci's Black Marx: Whither the Slave in Civil Society?," *Social Identities* 9. no. 2 (2003): 225–40.

17. David Marriott, *Whither Fanon? Studies in the Blackness of Being* (Redwood City, Calif.: Stanford University Press, 2018).

offers two possible resolutions: the first, that reason, law, and civil order might be redeemed through the enlargement of universal concepts, and the second, that they are irredeemable and therefore must be abandoned.

I aim instead to show how this supposed contradiction is inadequate to the breach. Freedom was defined not simply against slavery but through its universalization as collective mastery; civil order was defined not against brutish violence but through its internalization and legalization. Rather than accepting that the "civil orders" of colonial modernity relied on the elimination of disorder and violence, I want to draw attention to how they required its continued presence.

Explanations for anti-Black policing often swing between economic rationality and racialized violence.[18] The policing of Black lives is thought to operate *either* to shape exploitable subjects or to hasten their warehousing and disposability. I do not think we can "reduce" policing in this way. Positioning police as critical to the manufacture and protection of exploitation and inequality stops short of explaining how policing is embedded and entrenched across the world. Its violences are so built in to the normative ways that we think and order our existence that they are made practically mundane. Both abstract and intimate, the universality of Black policing is a normal part of Black life, as Walcott's epigraph to this chapter describes.

In Doreen Lawrence's words, murder is juxtaposed with the capture of labor, the police van with economic dependency: "everything in this country has Black people who have played a part in it." As such, rather than explanatory reduction, here we are drawn beyond logics of exploitation or/and disposability insofar as we are also drawn beyond the prison and police force. The potential for

18. Jackie Wang, *Carceral Capitalism* (South Pasadena, Calif.: Semiotext(e), 2018).

life in the Global North has continuously relied on slavery, colonial control, imperial expansion, and the hovering specter of anti-Black death. The world has been made hostile and uninhabitable for Black people as much as it is dependent on Blackness both materially and conceptually.

It is for this reason that slave society and colonial modernity more broadly were made in the image of police. The world formed in the image of police has been an attempt to manage and make sense of the tension between the drive to exterminate Black people and thus annihilate Blackness and simultaneously to maintain Blackness as a source of exploitable value and rights and privileges for whites. I will suggest that, born from the ongoing dependence of whiteness on an impossible drive toward anti-Black annihilation, police are less a thin blue line between civility and chaos and more the form of the world itself.

For this reason, I turn primarily to Barbados as the first Black slave society, as Hilary Beckles puts it, alongside a critical reading of Kant, Locke, and Hegel.[19] Both Barbados and the philosophical architects of modernity can be understood as attempts to construct a world from a frontier—to fuse a civil society without place for slave and Indigenous—from the furnace of a breach dependent on them. As such, I read Kant, Locke, and Hegel not so much as pioneering philosophers but as symptomatic of colonial modernity as well as recursively consolidating it. Throughout, I take the decisive attempt to consolidate the function of Black slavery *as* social order in British Barbados as a kind of microcosm of the world produced through colonial modernity. There the world formed in the image of police brought the prison and plantation together—with all whites becoming both prison guard and overseer. Policing is the normalization,

19. Hilary Beckles, "On Barbados, the First Black Slave Society," *Black Perspectives,* April 8, 2017, https://www.aaihs.org/on-barbados-the-first -Black-slave-society/.

internalization, and legalization of anti-Black and colonial violence that pervades the entire social fabric.

I do not intend this as an exhaustive account of policing's origins or logics, nor as a monocausal account that is simply reiterated across the contemporary world. I am, rather, interested in thinking with the spaces opened through the tensions and aporias of colonial modernity *as* white violence. Throughout, I am interested in examining the violences encoded within and practiced through white worlding. As such, I propose to consider, in chapter 1, the embedding of gratuitous violence in white civil society; in chapter 2, the property relation as policing; and in chapter 3, how both are entrenched through a continuous project of reform that sutures futurity under policing.

1. The World as Police

> If any poor small free-holder or other person kill a Negro or other Slave by Night, out of the Road or Common Path, and stealing, or attempting to steal his Provision, Swine, or other Goods, he shall not be accountable for it.
>
> —*An Act for the Governing of Negroes, Barbados, 1688*

JUST OVER A DECADE AFTER Stephen Lawrence's murder, Azelle Rodney was shot dead in a 2005 London Met police operation. Three police cars were used to block and ram the car in which Rodney was traveling before its tires were shot out. A police officer later identified as Anthony Long then shot Azelle eight times from fewer than two meters away. His body was left on the pavement for longer than sixteen hours while police-media mobilized a discourse of self-defense against a dangerous "gangster." Only after the family pushed for an inquiry were the police forced to admit that Rodney was unarmed. Witness testimony and incident data records showed that Rodney had not moved in the ways that Long had supposedly misconstrued as reaching for a gun. Footage of Rodney's murder was later released, in which officers can be heard saying "sweet as, sweet as" as he is executed.

With Wilderson, we might consider the vicious pleasures of Black deaths like Azelle's through the framework of *gratuitous* violence. This is a violence the irrational or libidinal excesses of which are considered fundamental to the cohering of civil society and the normative world.[1] Contrasted with forms of prejudice and

1. Biko Mandela Gray, "Frank Wilderson III," *Political Theology*

exploitation as comprehensible and contingent forms of violence that might be assuaged through police reforms and equality, gratuitous violence is both incoherent and necessary to the functioning of the world.[2]

Drawing attention to Wilderson's relegation of exploitation and material conditions in this explanation, his critics also claim ignorance of the disparate forms of racialization in colonial contexts.[3] But, in what follows, I show how the Barbados slave codes attempted to enforce a distinction between violence toward whites prompted by transgressions against prohibitions and law and violence toward Black slaves as gratuitous and without constraint.[4] In contrast with slaves, white servants were subject to law and contract through which relative freedoms could be gained and violence mediated. Moreover, the solidification of this distinction and the discharging of the enactment of gratuitous violence to all whites allowed for white civil society to coalesce.

In what follows, by staging a relationship between plantation Barbados and Immanuel Kant's Enlightenment, I suggest that the transformation from European frontier to established world required subjugating violence to be everywhere made pervasive and entrenched. Tiffany Lethabo King writes of how this gratuitous violence consolidated practices established prior even to

---

Network, September 21, 2021, https://politicaltheology.com/frank-wilderson-iii/.

2. Frank B. Wilderson III, "'We're Trying to Destroy the World': Anti-Blackness and Police Violence after Ferguson," November 2014, https://illwilleditions.noblogs.org/files/2015/09/Wilderson-We-Are-Trying-to-Destroy-the-World-READ.pdf.

3. Annie Olaloku-Teriba, "Afro-pessimism and the Logic of Anti-Blackness," *Historical Materialism* 26, no. 2 (2018): 96–122.

4. Frank B. Wilderson III, "The Black Liberation Army and the Paradox of Political Engagement," in *Postcoloniality–Decoloniality–Black Critique: Joints and Fissures,* ed. Sabine Broeck and Carsten Junker (Berlin: Campus, 2014), 204.

the Columbian crossing.[5] She draws on Wynter's account of how genocide and enslavement of the Indigenous in the Americas was preceded by African enslavement, sugar plantation structures, deracination, and slaughter. For example, in 1452, African slaves were used to work plantations on colonies like Madeira off the northwestern coast of Africa. These and later plantations on São Tomé provided a blueprint for the emergence and incubation of the plantation–slave complex that would later traverse the globe.[6]

Wynter suggests that the establishment of Black slavery prior to the Columbian crossing also rendered slavery a code that was embedded into the functioning of the world to which it gave rise.[7] Black slavery was significant for both setting in motion plantation economies that formed infrastructures of colonial capitalism but also symbolically consolidating African people as legitimately enslavable.[8] Africa and Africans become defined as void and absence: without laws, property, or reason, as "incapable of civilization," as Kant would later write.[9] Both materially and symbolically, African people became Black through violence and terror.[10] The "blackness produced through the worlding of 1492," as Keguro Macharia

5. Tiffany Lethabo King, *The Black Shoals: Offshore Formations of Black and Native Studies* (Durham, N.C.: Duke University Press, 2019). See Zakiyyah Iman Jackson, *Becoming Human* (New York: New York University Press, 2020), 112, on Black fungibility as condition of possibility for Kant.

6. Katherine McKittrick, "Plantation Futures," *Small Axe* 17, no. 3 (2013): 1–15.

7. Tapji Garba and Sara-Maria Sorentino, "Slavery Is a Metaphor: A Critical Commentary on Eve Tuck and K. Wayne Yang's 'Decolonization Is Not a Metaphor,'" *Antipode* 52, no. 3 (2020): 764–82, citing D. Scott and S. Wynter, "The Re-enchantment of Humanism: An Interview with Sylvia Wynter," *Small Axe* 8, no. 2 (2000): 119–207.

8. Garba and Sorentino.

9. Immanuel Kant, *Anthropology, History, Education,* ed. Günter Zöller and Robert Louden (Cambridge: Cambridge University Press, 2007).

10. Calvin Warren, *Ontological Terror: Blackness, Nihilism, and Emancipation* (Durham, N.C.: Duke University Press, 2018), 39. See G. Heng, *The Invention of Race in the European Middle Ages* (Cambridge: Cambridge University Press, 2018).

puts it, determined distinctions in violence made synonymous with the enslavement of Africans.[11]

I turn to Kant, together with how the slave codes were operationalized in constituting white society, because both are concerned with how a world can be constructed and sutured against a supposed frontier that threatens imminent destabilization.[12] The key to both was policing made irreducible to the institutions of political violence and criminalization because it was embedded into the nascent form of the world.[13] Where Wilderson insists that this violence is necessary for the world's coherence, the emphasis in what follows is also on how the necessary inclusion of Blackness in colonial modernity reveals that Blackness is produced primarily through a protective system for white civil society whose ultimate coherence is thereby rendered impossible. White civil society is held together through the pervasive drive to police as an attempt to suture a world that is reliant on that which it sets out to annihilate.

The transatlantic slave trade, colony, and plantation formed the coordinates for the consolidation of colonial modernity. In the process, the Caribbean basin became the engine of wealth for European shifts from mercantilism to industry.[14] Though white indentured

11. Keguro Macharia, "Belated: Interruption," *GLQ* 26, no. 3 (2020): 561–73.

12. While Kant's supposed anticolonialism has largely been practically orthodoxy, I am interested primarily in reading Kant's work in the context of attempted breach and suture (see note 66).

13. This conception of the world develops from Stefano Harney and Fred Moten, "Base Faith," *E-Flux Journal* 86 (2017); Frank B. Wilderson III, *Red, White, and Black: Cinema and the Structure of U.S. Antagonisms* (Durham, N.C.: Duke University Press, 2008); Palmer, "Otherwise"; Sylvia Wynter, "Unsettling the Coloniality of Being/Power/Truth/Freedom: Towards the Human, after Man, Its Overrepresentation—an Argument," *New Centennial Review* 3, no. 3 (2003): 257–337.

14. See Alexander Anievas and Kerem Nişancioğlu, *How the West Came to Rule: The Geopolitical Origins of Capitalism* (London: Pluto Press,

servants had been transported to the island since English settlement in 1627, Barbados's sugar mills and plantations were worked primarily by Black African slaves.

Growing and producing sugar was arduous and intensive. Forced to fertilize the land with excrement and urine, in conditions of starvation and grueling work that destroyed their hands, slaves were subject to painful work and early death. Tasks were monotonous, often using gang systems dividing and apportioning labor to maintain discipline. Slaves were whipped, tortured, and killed or worked to death. From underground incarceration in West African forts to the hold and the plantation, these were the sites of absolute subjugation and annihilation: around half of Barbados slaves required replacement every eight years.[15]

From within this furnace, the 1661 act later known as the slave codes legislated distinctions between servants and slave, with servants' rights codified and expanded. This made explicit in law distinctions between freemen, servants, and slaves that were already practiced. Rather than thinking of law as an edifice that makes explicit and codifies, I want to consider both what the codes implicitly express and rely on and the material and concrete capacities that are afforded through their abstractions, systems, and institutions.

Violence against indentured servants was mediated by law and tied to punishment, refusal to work, and rebellion. Working in continuity with and development of English labor and legal systems, the indentured had certain rights and could even take their masters to court. So, although the legal system was stacked against them in

---

2015); George Beckford, *Persistent Poverty: Underdevelopment in Plantation Economies of the Third World* (Kingston: University of the West Indies Press, 1972); Antonio Benítez-Rojo, *The Repeating Island: The Caribbean and the Postmodern Perspective* (Durham, N.C.: Duke University Press, 1996); Lisa Lowe, *The Intimacies of Four Continents* (Durham, N.C.: Duke University Press, 2015); Cedric Robinson, *Black Marxism: The Making of the Black Radical Tradition* (Chapel Hill: University of North Carolina Press, 2021).

15. Benítez-Rojo, *Repeating*, 70.

favor of the plantocracy, servants were subjects of contracts under English law. English indentured servants and convicts on average served fewer than seven years. Though treated severely, they were seen as workers whose bondage to work via contract could enable them to develop rationality and engage in civil order. In other words, underpinning the relationship between white servitude and legal community was a violence that was contingent on transgression and mediated by law and legal officers.

However, Black people stood outside of the law, while their control became the task of all whites.[16] That is to say, in contrast with the servant, Black slaves were positioned as object rather than subject of law and without the possibility of gaining freedom through work. Their relationship to violence was not mediated by contract—their existence was knitted together under direct force.[17]

The codes also explicitly consolidated slaves *as* Black, using *Negro* interchangeably with *slave*. Black people were described as a "heathenish brutish and an uncertain dangerous pride of people," setting up an attempted equivalency between violence, the Black person, and the slave. This confirms the breach in which, through transatlantic slavery, Black African people were, not figured in terms of complex relationship and difference, but written into the structure of this nascent world as a permanent state of nature: as waste, plague, and threat—as absolute evil, as Fanon wrote.[18]

Kant, whose work is so often seen as the pinnacle of modernity, provides the coordinates for thinking how the violence and alterity

16. Edward B. Rugemer, "The Development of Mastery and Race in the Comprehensive Slave Codes of the Greater Caribbean during the Seventeenth Century," *William and Mary Quarterly* 70, no. 3 (2013): 438. See also Simon P. Newman, *A New World of Labour: The Development of Plantation Slavery in the British Atlantic* (Philadelphia: University of Pennsylvania Press, 2013).

17. See Sexton, "Unbearable Blackness"; Wilderson, "Prison Slave."

18. Frantz Fanon, *The Wretched of the Earth* (New York: Grove, 2004).

produced through the breach could be brought under a lawlike system.[19] A principal problem for colonial modernity lay in its desire to control the relation with alterity such that its dependence on the violent inclusion of non-Europeans would not be destabilizing. Kant pointed to a solution that assumed coherence between the European subject and the world *insofar* as the world is limited to that which can be dominated and enclosed by that subject.

Though Kant (and the Enlightenment project) emphasize the novelty of alterity, this relationship with alterity must be managed to ensure that the subject of knowledge cannot be destabilized. In arguing for the synthetic a priori, he argues against both rationalism and empiricism that, though input from the world is necessary for the subject to develop new knowledge, that relationship must be mediated through an organizational framework. This framework delimits and conditions experience such that what can be known is limited by a transcendental structure of knowledge—a matrix of possible experience that is necessary for experience *as such*.[20] So, Kant writes that "the conditions of the possibility of experience in general are at the same time conditions of the possibility of the

19. See Michel Foucault, *History of Madness,* ed. Jean Khalfa, trans. Jonathan Murphy and Jean Khalfa (London: Routledge, 2006). An overview of scholarship on Kant and race is Robert Bernasconi, "Will the Real Kant Please Stand Up: The Challenge of Enlightenment Racism to the Study of the History of Philosophy," *Radical Philosophy* 117 (2003): 13–22.

20. Immanuel Kant, *Critique of Pure Reason,* ed. and trans. Paul Guyer and Allen Wood (Cambridge: Cambridge University Press, 2015). See Henry Allison, *Kant's Transcendental Idealism* (New Haven, Conn.: Yale University Press, 2004); Gary Banham, *Kant's Transcendental Imagination* (London: Palgrave Macmillan, 2005); Geoffrey Bennington, *Kant on the Frontier: Philosophy, Politics, and the Ends of the Earth* (New York: Fordham University Press, 2017); Jacques Derrida, "Force of Law: 'The Mystical Foundation of Authority,'" in *Deconstruction and the Possibility of Justice,* ed. Drucilla Cornell and Michael Rosenfeld (New York: Routledge, 1992); Patricia Kitcher, *Kant's Transcendental Psychology* (Oxford: Oxford University Press, 1990); Catherine Malabou, *Before Tomorrow: Epigenesis and Rationality* (Hoboken, N.J.: John Wiley, 2016).

objects of experience."[21] We experience the world as meaningfully ordered, as objects with persistence and in relation, because of an infrastructure of rules that determine the possibility of all objects of experience. Any new information is processed through this field of relations within which all empirical objects must be instantiated such that they can be known at all.

It is not that knowledge is predetermined by reason's laws (because we also require the addition of experience) but rather that the structuring boundaries of knowledge preshape the way that experience is processed. The idea is that we know the world through this framework, which domesticates alterity while the world is recursively defined through that domestication. We need alterity for that new knowledge to be "new," but the alterity of the new must be filtered through this framework so that there is no direct contact with the other's "otherness."[22] This world with which the subject has no contact then appears as delimited and organized insofar as it is constituted by the thinking subject themselves.[23] The assumption that the world must correlate to the subject is a process of synthesis in which the other is reduced to legibility with the European frame.

We thereby see the attempt to end contact with alterity *apart* from within the system produced under Europe. If the world Kant hopes for is "an island, enclosed by nature itself within unalterable limits,"[24] then, as Quill Kukla suggests, its orderliness is guarantee because our ordering faculties produce the island in the first place—"this island has no outside of the sort that could ever permeate or interrupt it."[25] This defined a chasm between alterity as it

21. Kant, *Critique,* A158/B197.

22. That this characterizes the entire critical and phenomenological tradition since; see Quentin Meillassoux, *After Finitude: An Essay on the Necessity of Contingency* (London: Bloomsbury, 2010).

23. Ashon Crawley, *Blackpentecostal Breath: The Aesthetics of Possibility* (New York: Fordham University Press, 2016), 116–17.

24. Kant, *Critique,* A235/B294.

25. Quill Kukla (writing as Rebecca), "The Antinomies of Impure Reason: Rousseau and Kant on the Metaphysics of Truth-Telling," *Inquiry* 48, no. 3 (2005): 226.

is inscribed within the matrix of possible experience and alterity that is rendered absolute—as unknowable and beyond the limits of possible assimilation.

Ashon Crawley writes of how the attempt to legislate on novelty is thus grounded on an impenetrable opacity, with Enlightenment thought dependent on the continued displacement of alterity to make possible a world of seeming coherence, calculability, and rationality.[26] As the slave is required for accumulation and transactions in which she are barred from involvement, so the "other" provides the conditions under which synthesis can produce a field of experience upon which it cannot impinge. The violence of the breach was both repudiated and filtered through a limiting process in which a calculable and quarantined "other" can appear as legible within the regime of colonial modernity.[27] The legislative architecture of experience is not the exclusion of difference but the attempt to pre-emptively annihilate and police the alterity upon which the system is dependent. In other words, the drive toward a unified world in correlation with thought is also the continued attempt to engineer a domain that is sutured against the alterity on which it depends.

Consider this movement constitutive of Kant's domesticated and quarantined alterity in conversation with plantation Barbados. Barbados indexes the attempt to establish a world through the suture of the breach. The transformation from European frontier to established world would write slaves into legible form through white enrichment.

In the interiorization of violence within law, reason, and the attempted knitting together of social order, a world made in common would be made in the congealing of whiteness through and

26. Crawley, *Blackpentecostal*, 121.

27. See Jackson, *Becoming*; Robbie Shilliam, "Decolonising the Grounds of Ethical Inquiry: A Dialogue between Kant, Foucault and Glissant," *Millennium* 39, no. 3 (2011): 649–65.

as policing. From a context in which white servants often worked alongside slaves, the collective subjection of slaves was the process through which whiteness cohered—deputizing white servants to capture runaway slaves and work as part of an emerging police force. Attempted marronage of slaves was common in the early seventeenth century. Richard Ligon's 1657 map of the island shows a European on horseback chasing two escapees in the same year that a "general hunting" day was called against fugitives. This unofficial vigilantism was in effect legislated for through the slave codes, becoming re-formed and reshaped as slave hunting in the form of white police.

Ratifying a collective responsibility for whites to control and capture slaves, patrols were formed to search slave quarters, chase runaways, and watch over gatherings like markets or ceremonies.[28] The codes proposed that surveillance systems be put in place, with a registry of plantation slaves and runaways. A ticketing system was used for slaves who were sent off-plantation, with those failing to provide them whipped and their masters fined. Servants who had completed their contracts were often employed by plantation owners to catch runaway slaves. Captured slaves could be lawfully whipped, have their noses slit or faces branded, or be executed, and if a master killed an African slave in the context of punishment, then no crime was committed. Punishments for indentured servants found off-plantation were significantly reduced, while the fee for capturing an African slave was increased, with any servant capturing a runaway granted relief from all future service.

The 1661 codes incentivized the murder of runaway slaves by their masters, because if a runaway slave was punished with death, the master would collect an indemnity against their loss of value. The laws did not warrant recompense for capture of the indentured,

28. Hilary Beckles, "From Land to Sea: Runaway Barbados Slaves and Servants, 1630–1700," *Slavery and Abolition* 6, no. 3 (1985): 79–94; Hadden, *Slave Patrols*; Michael Craton, *Sinews of Empire: A Short History of British Slavery* (New York: Anchor Books, 1974).

whereas capture of runaway slaves was rewarded with ten pounds of sugar for each mile the slave was escorted back to their master.[29] The later 1688 Act for the Governing of Negroes clarified this expansive form of policing in the suture of white order through the visceral presence of anti-Black violence: "if any poor small free-holder or other person kill a Negro or other Slave by Night, out of the Road or Common Path, and stealing, or attempting to steal his Provision, Swine, or other Goods, he shall not be accountable for it."[30]

It is clear here that the law preserved in the slave codes did not represent a coherent or rational world but rather a fraught and anxious transformation of brutish violence into a consolidated order oriented toward limit and proscription as rights and rule. Law- and police- making were central to the closure of the world around the continuation and redaction of abject violence. The slave codes entrenched civil society as a fraught system of threat, risk management, and viciousness.

The conscription of all white people to uphold authority over Black people, whether they owned slaves or not, was also the condition under which whites became subject to law in the possibility of transgression against it.[31] The consolidation of the plantocracy on Barbados allowed for violence to be remitted against servants and those who had completed their contracts (apart from legal transgressions against the plantation system). A nascent proletarianized class began to emerge insofar as the social whole was charged with enacting violence against Black people *without cause* or legal respite. Whiteness allowed access to land and resources through contract and completion of indenture but also through the collective policing of slaves. That is to say, the process of clarifying the rights of the

29. In Rugemer, "Development."
30. See also the discussion in Derica Shields, "In the Aftermath of Slavery, British Police Still Know Whom to Target," *Frieze*, September 2020.
31. Nikil Pal Singh points to how relationships between policing and security were instrumental to how "whiteness coalesced as a political subjectivity." Singh, "Whiteness," 1092.

indentured under the law was one and the same process through which anti-Black violence was made not only permissible for all whites but actively prescribed.

The legal and social practices that consolidated a regime of violence against the slave (with no status within the world under creation) simultaneously functioned to enable the accumulation of rights and capacities for all whites. The codes wrote in to law a group not only protected under its rights but, in the same process, deputized to police all others. As Wilderson suggests, we see here that civil society coalesced around violence against Black people.[32] The violence of contact with Black people figured as state of nature was the vehicle through which normativity—of legitimated violence, law, civility, the European—became possible.[33] This follows Tea Troutman's assertion that "it is the slave which precedes the colony/nation-state, and not the colonial order that produces the slave."[34]

All whites were to enforce the codes through surveillance and coercion, being required to live on or enter plantations and search quarters, as well as inflicting punishment and martial law on suspected runaway slaves and those found without passes. The consolidation of colonial order as white community was the creation of a collective police force. A world in common had congealed as if a skein had been pulled over abject violence in an attempt to suture and ground.

The world produced is not contingently one of anti-Black containment. Rather, consolidating a world as suture of the breach is necessarily dependent on subjugating violence everywhere made pervasive and entrenched. This world's seeming stability was pro-

32. Selamawit D. Terrefe, "On *Afropessimism* by Frank B. Wilderson III," *Georgia Review*, Winter 2020, https://thegeorgiareview.com/posts/on -afropessimism-by-frank-b-wilderson-iii/.

33. We should be careful to distinguish this claim from a broader point that the formation of liberal order has required the legitimation of violence as within the nation-state. See Derrida, "Force."

34. Tea Troutman, "The Border Crisis of the Migrant-Slave," *Wear Your Voice*, September 28, 2021, https://wyvarchive.com/the-border-crisis -of-the-migrant-slave/.

duced through incessant work against threat, fractious and vulnerable. If Black people became Black insofar as they were subject to gratuitous violence, then white people became white through the knotted tensions of desire to be the police, to be beyond the police, and to be policed.

I want to think about the implications of the embedding and universalization of this white collective mastery in the constitution of freedom. Many Enlightenment accounts invoke the image of the slave as negative infraction of liberty, with freedom defined as self-possession.[35] Kant (following Rousseau) is primarily concerned to think of autonomy as mastery over the state of nature such that it cannot possibly bleed into the realm of law, reason, and order. As such, he requires that autonomy have no source other than universalized reason: "it is requisite to reason's lawgiving that it should need to presuppose only *itself*, because a rule is objectively and universally valid only when it holds without the contingent, subjective conditions that distinguish one rational being from another."[36] For Kant, we are autonomous reasoning beings insofar as we are bound to rules of our own making.

But, while reason's prerequisite is the absolute disconnection between the space of reasons and the space of causes, it turns out that this disconnection must be unendingly policed. In brief, ensuring that such rules are universally valid relies on "the subjection of inclination to the rule of reason and its demand for universalizability."[37] The autonomy of reason is thus set against corruption by

35. Denise Ferreira Da Silva, "Toward a Black Feminist Poethics: The Quest(ion) of Blackness toward the End of the World," *Black Scholar* 44, no. 2 (2014): 81–97.

36. Immanuel Kant, *Practical Philosophy*, ed. and trans. M. Gregor (Cambridge: Cambridge University Press, 1996), 5:21.

37. Paul Guyer, "Freedom: Will, Autonomy," in *Immanuel Kant: Key Concepts—a Philosophical Introduction*, ed. W. Dudley, 85–102 (Stocksfield, U.K.: Acumen, 2010).

the particular, contingent, and subjective. For Kant, it is possible to escape the *metaphorical* slavery of inclination and external intrusion on our actions by nurturing and enforcing rationality and decreasing the power of that which lies outside it, which is to say, the state of nature. If freedom is sutured to order and ordering as the condition of being in the world, then one becomes free only under submission to law and limit and in vigilance against the insurgency of nature and desire. The frontier is at once universalized and internalized.

Because, for Kant, anybody existing outside of a (European) nation-state embodies the state of nature, they represent a threat to order. As he writes, "[somebody] in the state of nature deprives me of this security; even if he doesn't do anything to me—by the mere fact that he isn't subject to any law and is therefore a constant threat to me."[38] Forever in the state of nature, Black people are positioned not simply as antithesis to the lawful subject whose freedom would be guaranteed under a social order thought to be produced through lawfulness. In other words, Black and Indigenous people—slaves and colonized—were a perpetual threat.[39] The threat is not limited to political sovereignty but, as disordering alterity, could open out thought and law—destabilizing both—and so also undoing freedom.[40]

In this sense, the Kantian policing of reason is also a war against that which lies outside of seeming rational control.[41] Our relationship with the "other," for Kant, is supposedly set up as an a priori

38. Immanuel Kant, *Political Writings*, ed. and trans. Donna Brinton and Janet Goodwin (Cambridge: Cambridge University Press, 1991), 73.

39. Richard Slotkin, *Regeneration through Violence: The Mythology of the American Frontier, 1600–1860* (Norman: University of Oklahoma Press, 2000).

40. In part, Kant's concern in conjoining freedom with mastery is due to what remains from Hobbes in that the state of nature is *spectral*—it is omnipresent in its possible return and "threatened regression." Mary Nyquist, *Arbitrary Rule: Slavery, Tyranny, and the Power of Life and Death* (Chicago: University of Chicago Press, 2013), 260.

41. Scott, *Conscripts*, 13.

disconnection from that alterity that could sway the subject from law and norm. But, in fact, this relationship is required to be one of perpetual suspicion, policing, defense, and disavowal. This requires an endless struggle against that which is disordering and pathological and which is ensconced in those "lawless savages" who, for Kant, have a fundamental incapacity to think.[42] The space of representation (the world) and the freedoms available within it, while supposedly produced *as* and *through* a rule-like matrix, thus results from incessant policing. What emerges as the space of reasons and freedom, to follow Anthony Farley, is the form of repressed desire and violence.[43] Rather than accepting the absence of law in violence, and the absence of violence in law, policing is fundamental to the operations of law and norm and its attempted repression.

Superficially, this line of thought parallels Foucault's. For example, Foucault similarly accepts that freedom is interwoven with policing, where policing is the form that the social world takes. Moreover, law as the expression of sovereign power is submerged and internalized within modernity's "code of normalization."[44] This dispersal of policing through normalization and channeling of behavior operates as an ordering function that works as a kind of historicized version of Kant's transcendental, rather than as a kind of repression of disorder (i.e., a thin blue line).[45]

However, not only does the Foucauldian reduction threaten to detooth our understanding of policing so that it cannot adequately deal with abject violence and state murders like Azelle Rodney's but, as Alexander Weheliye details, this reading of modernity is sanitized

42. Kant, *Political*, 45–49.

43. Anthony P. Farley, "Accumulation," *Michigan Journal of Race and Law* 11 (2005): 60; see James Trafford, "Re-engineering Commonsense," *Glass Bead*, 2017, https://www.glass-bead.org/article/re-engineering -commonsense/.

44. Michel Foucault, *Society Must Be Defended: Lectures at the Collège de France, 1975–76* (London: Penguin, 2004), 38.

45. See Melayna Lamb, *A Philosophical History of Police Power* (London: Bloomsbury, 2023).

from colonial domination and violence.[46] This leads Foucault to assume an ontology of the social across which hierarchy is distributed, rather than to acknowledge how Blackness was produced through violence as its necessarily incommensurable exterior. Hence Foucault is concerned with a European subject confronted with power, subject to social force, and compelled toward self-policing, while simultaneously "naturalizing racial difference by placing 'other' races outside Europe."[47]

For example, Black people were legible to colonial modernity as naturalized and permanent slave: "Americans and negroes cannot govern themselves. Thus are good only as slaves."[48] Black people, according to Kant, "have by nature no feeling that rises above the ridiculous," and so, without "capacity to act in accordance with concepts and principles," they are by nature not just unfree but beyond even the possibility of freedom.[49] Here, as Ronald Judy argues, Kant makes an illegitimate appeal to a transcendental account of Blackness, so operating as a necessary condition of thought itself.[50] In disavowing this condition of Kant's modernity, Foucault repeats the Kantian disavowal of the exterior on which the space of reason (or the space of norms) relies.

As a result, Foucault follows Kant in suggesting that there is no "outside" to the space of power, which is exercised "only over free subjects, and only insofar as they are free," so disavowing the possibility of a radical exterior to the social realm.[51] In the sugges-

46. Alexander Weheliye, *Habeas Viscus: Racializing Assemblages, Biopolitics, and Black Feminist Theories of the Human* (Durham, N.C.: Duke University Press, 2014).

47. Weheliye, 59.

48. Kant, as cited in Mark Larrimore, "Sublime Waste: Kant on the Destiny of the 'Races,'" *Canadian Journal of Philosophy* 29, no. 1 (1999): 99–125.

49. Kant, *Anthropology,* 2:253.

50. Ronald Judy, "Kant and the Negro," *Surfaces* 1 (1991).

51. Michel Foucault, "The Subject and Power," *Critical Inquiry* 8, no. 4 (1982): 790.

tion that the social is carceral, then, Foucault repeats the Kantian exclusion of that which is required for the social to exist, while dissolving collective social and state domination and abjection into circulations of power. As Joy James writes,

> in *Discipline and Punish* Foucault remains mute about the incarcerated person's vulnerability to police beatings, rape, shock treatments, and death row. Penal incarceration and executions are the state's procedures for discarding the unassimilable into an external inferno of nonexistence.[52]

Where Foucault considers how policing coalesces into norms that form webs of meaning and control, we see here that this normative structure is possible only through the ongoing reproduction and disavowal of a prophylactic blockage of an exterior that is its prerequisite. The normative world shaped by policing has, as its requirement, a violence to protect its boundaries while those boundaries are simultaneously held together and obscured by that violence. Foucault's "dark Kantianism" cannot see, therefore, how the structure of the world relies on and reproduces a normalized social field whose stabilization results from an endless requirement of violence.

The presupposition and naturalization of Black people as slaves in Kant's work allow for the continuation of violence under collective and legal formations of the kind exemplified earlier, while that violence is made unthinkable *as* violence because it is prerequisite for rational autonomy. As Farley suggests, "reason, then, has a politics that looks like lawlessness, chaos, havoc, a war of all against all."[53] The supposed impurities of subjective inclination, desire, and concrete particularity index an insecurity in the structure of autonomy that always must be staved off: the fantasies

52. Joy James, *Resisting State Violence: Radicalism, Gender, and Race in U.S. Culture* (Minneapolis: University of Minnesota Press, 1996).

53. Anthony Paul Farley, "Reason's Lure: The Enchantment of Subordination: The Dream of Interpretation," *University of Miami Law Review* 57 (2003): 696.

and material realities of anti-Black violence are both inscribed and redacted from within the structures of reason itself.[54]

With freedom set against a metaphorical slavery, the violences of slavery were disavowed in the same moment as collective subjection was consolidated. As such, the mass manumission of slaves cohered toward what Guyora Binder terms the "slavery of emancipation."[55] For instance, Barbados did not have enough land for emancipated Black people to work anywhere other than on the plantations where they had been enslaved. Practically all its 166 square miles were organized into sugar estates. After emancipation, the "free" were required to endure arduous labor without recompense and to remain on the sites of the plantations while under contract of apprenticeships. Perhaps predictably, then, as Caree Banton describes, apprentices were subject to constant surveillance, control, and heavily conditional freedoms.[56] Black people were faced with a barrage of laws restricting movement that were supposed to help them "realize" that they would be best simply living and working on their former plantations.[57]

Across emancipation, as I discuss in chapter 3, there remained a core requirement for whites to keep control over Black people. Widespread but relatively low-level strikes had taken place in 1838, with workers refusing contracts and working conditions. One result was the 1840 Contract Law, which effectively bound laborers to

54. See Celia Brickman, *Aboriginal Populations in the Mind: Race and Primitivity in Psychoanalysis* (New York: Columbia University Press, 2003).

55. G. Binder, "The Slavery of Emancipation," *Cardozo Law Review* 17 (1995): 2063.

56. Caree Banton, "More Auspicious Shores: Post-emancipation Barbadian Emigrants in Pursuit of Freedom, Citizenship, and Nationhood in Liberia, 1834–1912" (PhD diss., Vanderbilt University, 2013), https://ir .vanderbilt.edu/bitstream/handle/1803/12772/BANTON.pdf.

57. Bruce M. Taylor, "Black Labor and White Power in Post-emancipation Barbados: A Study of Changing Relationships," *A Current Bibliography on African Affairs* 6, no. 2 (1973): 186.

plantations, transforming the supposedly "free wage worker into a 'located' plantation tenant."[58] The law attempted to keep laborers working on plantations and allowed that they could be imprisoned or made homeless from the tied "chattel houses" if they were found to be insubordinate or not to be working in accord with the planter's desires. With the prospect of earning higher wages on nearby colonies, at the end of apprenticeship, Black people did begin to emigrate. This immediately prompted calls to save the island from desertion and eventually led to the 1836 Emigration Act of Barbados.[59] In writing the act, Barbadian planters, in conjunction with the British, barred recruitment by potential employers and endeavored to imprison former slaves on the island.[60]

The island's boundaries were traversed with an expansive apparatus of surveillance and control.[61] Plantation and prison frequently became practically one and the same, with people often ending up working in the same spaces from which they had been removed. With approximately 501 apprentices per square mile, emancipation ensured the perpetuation of Barbados itself as "an island prison."[62] Postslave society saw the expansion of policing and laws restricting the movement of Black people. As such, Walcott considers that emancipation did not allow formerly enslaved people to move from their surroundings; they were instead faced with laws against idleness, vagrancy, and movement, all of which extended their enclosure.[63]

This governance of Black people reads as distinct from slavery only if we also accept that emancipation recapitulated the supposed

58. Beckles, cited in Dawn P. Harris, *Punishing the Black Body: Marking Social and Racial Structures in Barbados and Jamaica* (Athens: University of Georgia Press, 2017), 100.

59. Minutes of the Legislative Council, March 3, 1840, cited in Taylor, "Black," 184.

60. Taylor, 95.

61. Harris, *Punishing,* 102.

62. Taylor, "Black," 183.

63. Walcott, *Long,* 37.

colonial movement from state of nature to civil society. Instead, with policing the form of civil society, this inscription of violence into the production of normativity and social life became etched into the desires and pleasures of whiteness and recoded under law and reason. As slave society was transformed into postslavery colony, the equivalency set up in law of Black person with slave and chattel was definitively extended to the "criminal." The extension was already implicit in the codes, becoming consolidated insofar as criminalization became the condition of possibility of Black movement and antagonism toward collective property regimes. To be a little more precise, that Black people were equivalent with "criminal" was palpable wherever they attempted to exercise freedoms going beyond the condition of the slave.

With formal abolition and emancipation, the criminal became a central technology through which the functional relation of the slave could be preserved in Barbados. The translation of brutish violence under law, as Saidiya Hartman describes, had invalidated enslaved people's agency in the same moment that agency was recognized only insofar as it took the form of criminality.[64] The criminalization of slave resistance was written into being both as pervasive atmosphere of potential disorder and as contingent eruptions of rebellion. It is within this hovering tension and threat that the criminal emerged not only as an omnipresent threat of disorder and chaos but primarily as a way of making legible the functional position of the slave in a domesticated, imperialist environment.

The role of a nascent formalized criminal justice system was to create substantive linkages between Black people and plantation labor. This rested on the idea of ingrained criminality without possibility of redemption: the emancipated were effectively made criminal, with the embodiment of criminality evident insofar as they attempted to operate in any role other than that of the slave. To follow Farley, Black criminality becomes part of the means through

64. Hartman, *Scenes*, 80.

which slavery is *perfected*—that is to say, transformed, embedded, and disavowed—within civil society:

> The movement from slavery to segregation to neosegregation is the movement of slavery perfecting itself. White-over-black is neosegregation. White-over-black is segregation. White-over-black is slavery.[65]

The alleged antinomy I discussed at the start of this book resonates wherever attention is drawn to how so-called liberal democracies are ceaselessly violent. Many writers have sought to consider whether Kant's purported universalism unravels under the weight of partiality given his statements regarding Black and Indigenous people. The Enlightenment project is then charged either with a radical anticolonial cosmopolitanism or the imposition of universalizing hegemony across Europe's colonial expansion.[66]

65. Anthony P. Farley, "Perfecting Slavery," *Loyola University of Chicago Law Journal* 36 (2004): 222.

66. I return to these issues in chapter 3, but, e.g., see Sankar Muthu's sweeping attempt to rehabilitate Kantian cosmopolitanism as cohering with anticolonial movements. Muthu, *Enlightenment against Empire* (Princeton, N.J.: Princeton University Press, 2003). This suggests that Kant desired equal worth for all people even against evidence that this is never applied to subjugated people. Pauline Kleingeld famously suggests that Kant's later work exonerates his earlier statements on the basis that he moved away from racial hierarchy. Kleingeld, "Kant's Second Thoughts on Race," *Philosophical Quarterly* 57, no. 229 (2007): 573–92. See also Oliver Eberl, "Kant on Race and Barbarism: Towards a More Complex View on Racism and Anti-colonialism in Kant," *Kantian Review* 24, no. 3 (2019): 385–413. See Alan J. Kellner, "States of Nature in Immanuel Kant's Doctrine of Right," *Political Research Quarterly* 73 (2019): 727–39, for a position that shows Kant's argument regarding the rights of possession to provide colonialist justification, while suggesting that this may be accommodated within a Kantian framework. Charles W. Mills suggests that these seemingly contradictory positions within Kant's work can be reconciled if we understand Kant as regarding Black people as subhuman. Mills, "Kant's *Untermenschen,*" in *Black Rights/White Wrongs: The Critique of Racial Liberalism,* 91–112 (New York: Oxford Academic, 2017). A collec-

Instead, I have shown that the so-called freedoms of colonial modernity not only depended on the unfreedoms of others but produced a world in which others' freedoms cannot even be figured. This reading is at odds with any criticism of Kant as excluding non-Europeans from a universalizing account of reason and civility. Because the violences of the state of nature exist prior to the supposed order of freedom and law, Kant is, instead, driven by the desire to show that Europeans are exempted from that violence such that reason and law may be secured for them. This shifts focus toward how alterity was both produced as infinite threat and domesticated as a function that continues to stabilize colonial order as policing.

In Kant and Barbados, the problem of the frontier is resolved through preemptive immunity from contingency and disorder.[67] If the idea of the thin blue line depends on the manufacture and protection from a remainder of violent alterity inscribed along frontiers, here that frontier would be internalized such that the breach is sutured a priori. But as we've seen, any redemption from disorder required to preemptively sever colonial modernity from absolute alterity is recovered only through the incessant limiting of the world against a supposedly inherent and immovable evil whose impossible absorption is the true ground of reason. This allowed reason to seem to be its own progenitor and legislator by determining boundaries that are internalized to ensure that danger, threat, and chaos are voided, because no thing can lie outside the world as relational totality.

In staging a relationship between Barbados and Kant's Enlightenment, we have seen the prefiguration of the distribution of

tion of essays providing a thorough overview of this scholarship is Katrin Flikschuh and Lea Ypi, eds., *Kant and Colonialism: Historical and Critical Perspectives* (Oxford: Oxford University Press, 2014). In practically all of this work, there is little to no reflection of the ramifications of Kant's belief that Black people are incapable of autonomy and self-governance, ensuring both the justification of colonialism and the impossibility of their inclusion in the category of universal humanity.

67. Kukla, "Antinomies," 227.

violent relationships between master and slave, conquistador-settler and Indigenous, becoming embedded into the structure of civil society.[68] The supposed absorption of the slave into legal frameworks was the precondition for its continuation and afterlives, while the naturalization of slavery as equivalent with Black people made them unthinkable as part of social relations.[69] This is to say, the *attempted* universalization of mastery remains an unthinkable presupposition of an imagined social order whose brutish violence could thereby be analytically known and affectively felt as rational and lawful.

As David Marriott describes, Blackness is "both excluded and imperiously demanded by Western reason."[70] Attending to the Barbadian context centers how intimate tensions of dependency and annihilation confirm that any attempted suture of slave society also indexes not just the possibility but also the *impossibility* of that social order. A white world of order and rule is not possibly completable in the presence of Blackness that cannot be eliminated. Blackness does not operate as "other" in antithesis to this world but as ever-present crisis. Colonial modernity is reliant on violent inclusion within a global order whose completion is thereby made impossible—the alterity on which Kant's entire project relies is that which it must preemptively annihilate. If there is no place in the world for those upon whom the world depends, then these relationships of dependency are a fragile setup that simultaneously requires the annihilation and the multiplication of enslaved people.[71]

68. Wilderson, *Red,* 80. The phrase "conquistador-settler" is from Lethabo King, *Black*.

69. See Sara-Maria Sorentino, "The Abstract Slave: Anti-Blackness and Marx's Method," *International Labor and Working-Class History* 96 (2019): 17–37; Michel-Rolph Trouillot, *Silencing the Past: Power and the Production of History* (Boston: Beacon Press, 1995).

70. David Marriott, *Lacan Noir: Lacan and Afro-pessimism* (London: Palgrave Macmillan, 2021), 122.

71. Abdul JanMohamed, *Manichean Aesthetics: The Politics of Literature in Colonial Africa* (Amherst: University of Massachusetts Press, 1989).

The preservation of whiteness—of what is considered civility, rationality, freedom—requires the interminable production and policing of Blackness. Tyrone Palmer, drawing on Césaire, elucidates this tension:

> Blackness functions as the raw material of the World, as what makes the World possible even as it is denied a place or ground within it. . . . the World, as a metonym for colonial modernity, is in a very material sense built on the expropriation of Black labor (in the material and psychic senses), while also being marked by Blackness more broadly as its constitutive outside. . . . Europe's domination of and through the World depends on Blackness occupying its underside.[72]

What resulted was the formation of a collective order on a foundational aporia—the violence of this staving off of genocide, an endless protraction of what Fanon points to as a *perpetual* yet necessarily "incomplete death."[73]

Consider the mechanisms through which this protracted genocide can persist—of deracination, hyperexploitation, dispossession, extinction—while naturalized, redacted, and forged into the stability of a supposedly liberal world order. In protracted genocide, this world is required to continually relate to that which is constitutively destabilizing. Here proximities and segregations are enfolded under the incessant displacement of violent relation by filtering the terms of that relation through absolute control (domestication) and absolute alterity (generative disorder). The breach continues to provide purpose in filtration, regulation, and limitation to produce a world whose incapacity to process contingency, alterity, and plenitude is its supposed advantage.[74]

The resulting staving off of genocide produces a species of violence and vehemence against those whose spectral presence

72. Palmer, "Otherwise," 253.

73. Frantz Fanon, *A Dying Colonialism,* trans. H. Chevalier and A. Gilly (New York: Grove Press, 1967).

74. See Da Silva, "Toward."

haunts the Kantian thought–world relationship.[75] The world is produced not only as horizon of possibility but as cage. As such, this self-imposed incarceration, as Kukla puts it, indexes not only the mastery of a specific and secure domain but also a drive toward imperial re-creation as global subjugation.[76] This had set in motion a containment strategy as program of domination: colonial modernity required that police have no determinable limit across our carceral island world.

We learn from Barbados that the slave functioned to knit together whiteness through the relation of supposedly absolute submission and discretionary violence from all whites. Where the rights of whiteness were conferred in distributed and collective subjection, Blackness was positioned as everywhere a negation and threat to whiteness. Barbados clarifies how the violence productive of a white community as police became legible by redacting the violence through which the slave was made perpetually outside of the domain of civil society. The collective subjection engendering "the submission of the slave to all whites"[77] was the means through which "whites" as collective order would be crafted.

However, while considering, with Wilderson, how that violence has been necessary to the world's coherence, I have also emphasized how this world becomes meaningful only insofar as it is unable to confront its own inevitable negation. The coherence of meaning itself comes undone through the very conditions supposed to provide that coherence. The insecurity at the core of the regulative world undoes the assertion of the categorical world from the ground up.[78] While the supposed limits of thought are folded back onto a world

75. Jackson, *Becoming,* 112.

76. Jackson, 225.

77. Hartman, *Scenes,* 24.

78. Sean Gaston, *The Concept of World from Kant to Derrida* (New York: Rowman and Littlefield, 2013), 115.

thus supposedly given integrity, this resultantly unsuturable form is saturated with failure. What is required, therefore, is a constant distraction by "symbolic fears and punishments," as David Marriott puts it.[79] And so, as Marriott suggests, whiteness acts as "safeguard against any confusion or panic and precisely because it is irredeemably exposed to both at the level of need and desire."[80] This is not to reify whiteness but rather to note that its aporetic convolutions intertwine to produce fractious panic and insecurity *as conditions* of an unachievable security.

Insofar as whiteness is incapable of forming a world (because Kant's island is a mirage), the matrix productive of experience is then neither a metaphysical nor a transcendental structure—it is an arrangement of life whose form is police. The security of meaning and law, progress and reason, is a fantasy whose possibility and impossibility is violence. Born through a preemptive retreat, white-security-as-worlding is incorrigibly grounded in the Blackness it ceaselessly produces and abjures. The desires of whiteness are thus arranged in the form of anti-Blackness such that incessant policing is mistaken for privilege and pleasure.

Despite Kant's pretensions, we see that this world and its worlding—however it appears—is not a coherent, stable, and civil order: it is held together as police. Because the literal blood and sand of the colonized continue to be the grounds of white life, the continuation and consolidation of violence and terror form productive conditions of our world and white kinship within it. This has required the omnipresence of police built into the formation of society and the world itself.

We have been forced to partake in worlds of subjection—a modernity dream in which freedoms index collective mastery, justice indexes depravity, and reason indexes the fractious indexing of thought to a myopic world. Policing reaches into the ways sub-

---

79. Marriott, *Lacan*, 147.
80. Marriott, 151.

jectivities have been formed in control, scrutiny, and limit. What results is a situation in which we cannot practically experience or even imagine worlds free from policing. Within this world, freedom is a cage.

2. Property Is a Plantation

Negroes [are] an heathenish brutish and an unsertaine dangerous kinde of people . . . yett wee well know by the right rule
of reason and order wee are not to leave them to the Arbitrary
cruele and outragious wills of every evill disposed person but
soo farr to protect them as wee doo many other goods and Chattles and alsoe somewhat farther as being created Men though
without the Knowledge of God in the world.

—*An Act for the Better Ordering and Governing of Negroes, 1661*

THIS CHAPTER FOLLOWS along the track set out by Antony Farley's
statement that the system of property is a plantation is not metaphorical.[1] I suggest that the codes that bound white collectives as
police were also an aftereffect of the collective formation of property
regimes requiring planters and servants to act together as protective
tissue. Property, then, is primarily a relation between people that
later became processed through the lens of owner and commodity.[2]

Yet, as I mentioned earlier, policing is often characterized as
the thin blue line of property protection. For example, while many
recent approaches attend to relationships between police and colonial history, these center how policing was required to protect
property regimes produced through colonization.[3] The suggestion

1. Farley, "Perfecting." See also McKittrick, "Plantation."
2. Farley, "Accumulation," 69.
3. Vicky Osterweil, *In Defense of Looting: A Riotous History of Uncivil
Action* (New York: Bold Type Books, 2020), 17; Singh, "Whiteness"; Alex
Vitale, "The Best Way to 'Reform' the Police Is to Defund the Police,"

is that policing was set up as the violent arm of racial capitalism, buoyed by claims regarding the historical birth of the police as a force to maintain plantocratic power.[4] Property, for these approaches, is necessarily understood as a system of rights over land and commodities that guarantees ownership as excludability of others. This understanding of property orbits around (critiques of) the widespread view of the consolidation of colonial property regimes in the mid-seventeenth century most associated with the work of John Locke, sometimes known as the father of liberalism.

Against the Lockean view, I suggest that in the moment that the frontier was shaped into an emerging capitalist world, the violences that became embedded into white social relations produced through slavery were one and the same as the property relation.[5] I draw attention to the ways that Locke's justification for colonization as necessarily annihilating the state of nature in fact required the continued presence of the state of nature as slave. Concentrating on the interweaving of police, property, and the function of slavery highlights how the consolidation of whiteness through the collective subjection of Black people simultaneously functioned as collective possession. Put bluntly, policing cannot be reduced to colonial property protection because property and policing coincide.

The point here is not (only) that an emergent liberalism was coextensive with the plantation but rather that its primary concern (as with Kant) was to transform a frontier into a world through the

Jacobin, June 3, 2020, https://jacobinmag.com/2020/06/defund-police -reform-alex-vitale.

4. Marlese Durr, "What Is the Difference between Slave Patrols and Modern Day Policing? Institutional Violence in a Community of Color," *Critical Sociology* 41, no. 6 (2015): 875; Philip McHarris, "Disrupting Order: Race, Class, and the Roots of Policing," in *Violent Order: Essays on the Nature of Police,* ed. David Correia and Tyler Wall, 31–52 (Chicago: Haymarket Press, 2021).

5. I did not have a chance to think with it before finalizing this book, but Denise Ferreira Da Silva navigates adjacent ground in *Unpayable Debt* (New York: Sternberg Press, 2022).

internalization, domestication, and disavowal of slavery and its violences. These violences were continued through the management of the tensions inherent in a social order built on proximity with those who are required for the ongoing production of property regimes while being barred from access to them. As Fanon emphatically stated, "Europe is literally the creation of the Third World."[6] Capitalism today continues to depend on those Black, Indigenous, and colonized people whose lives and labor are expropriated across the world.

The slave codes characterized slaves as chattel property, something that beforehand had not required explicit law because it was so entrenched in custom and practice.[7] In the process, long-established forms of violence became prescribed in law and have four essential characteristics: lifetime status, that the status of slave follows the mother, racial identification, and slave as chattel.[8] While these characteristics followed English legal concepts typically applied to chattel as exchangeable commodity, slaves were also subject to legal concepts of real estate that were distinct in English law.[9] Left implicit in the codes, their prescription emerges in formulations of the use of slaves for bequeathment in wills and deeds of sale, as gifts, for payment, as loan security, and as plantation inventory.[10] Slaves functioned as both fungible commodity and sources of further finan-

6. Fanon, *Wretched*, 81.

7. Jerome Handler, "Custom and Law: The Status of Enslaved Africans in Seventeenth-Century Barbados," *Slavery and Abolition* 37, no. 2 (2016): 240.

8. Handler, 236.

9. Barbados heralded the "breakdown of the ancient distinction between real and chattel property during the colonial period." K-Sue Park, "Conquest and Slavery as Foundational to Property Law," Georgetown Law Faculty Publications, 2021, 47.

10. Handler, "Custom," 16.

cial accumulation through widespread English investment and collateral, while also forming an enduring source of inherited labor.[11]

Let us first consider how foregrounding chattel and labor (rather than fungibility) coheres with the colonial labor theory of property at the core of Locke's ideas, in which property is made through the transformation of land by labor upon it:

> Whatsoever [one] removes out of the State that Nature hath provided, and left it in, he hath mixed his Labor with, and joined to it something that is his own, and thereby makes it his Property.[12]

This state of nature prior to civility was identified with African and what later became known as American land and Indigenous people. For Locke, this made possible the preparing of land for property relations as terra nullius, as well as a people not only fit for enslavement but morally requiring mastery. Land and people in the state of nature would be appropriated and reorganized into regimes of property through the improvement of that land by human action upon it:

> As much Land as a Man Tills, Plants, Improves, Cultivates, and can use the Product of, so much is his Property. He by his Labor does, as it were, inclose it from the Common.[13]

The reality, as Robert Nichol polemically suggests, is that property relations are thus generated by theft.[14] In the work of Locke, property is made as a regime of rights over homelands and personhood through collective expropriation and labor. For Locke, colonization is a process of cultivation to improve land to its best

---

11. Richard Pares, *Merchants and Planters,* Economic History Review Supplement 4 (New York: Cambridge University Press, 1960).

12. John Locke, *Two Treatises* (1689), V §27.

13. Locke, V §32.

14. Robert Nichols, *Theft Is Property! Dispossession and Critical Theory* (Durham, N.C.: Duke University Press, 2020). See also Laura Brace, *The Politics of Property: Labor, Freedom, and Belonging* (New York: Palgrave Macmillan, 2004).

potential. Not only is this supposedly vindicated by God's will but it is also a requirement upon the colonizer to redeem land from being "wasted":

> God gave the world to men in common; but since he gave it them for their benefit, and the greatest conveniences of life they were capable to draw from it, it cannot be supposed he meant it should always remain common and uncultivated. He gave it to the use of the industrious and rational, (and labor was to be his title to it).[15]

Under the moral requirements of natural law, any wasted land should be developed and made productive. Preexisting forms of cultivation and commerce were disavowed and destroyed, and legitimate possession was formed as a relationship that could be produced only by the colonizer. Land not cultivated by empire was understood as waste, with only the colonizer capable of shepherding the transformation of nature into property.[16]

Indigenous people were excluded from property rights because they were seen as an integral part of that nature in a state of waste. They were rationally dispossessed by their own state of nature—a "people arrested in their evolution, impervious to reason, incapable of directing their own affairs," as Fanon later describes this colonial projection.[17] On these grounds, Indigenous people were not seen as benign—they also required "improvement" through the force of

---

15. Locke, *Two Treatises,* II §34. See also Vinay Gidwani and Rajyashree N. Reddy, "The Afterlives of 'Waste': Notes from India for a Minor History of Capitalist Surplus," *Antipode* 43, no. 5 (2011): 1625–58; Ellen Meiksins Wood, *Empire of Capital* (London: Verso Books, 2003).

16. Brenna Bhandar, *Colonial Lives of Property: Law, Land, and Racial Regimes of Ownership* (Durham, N.C.: Duke University Press, 2018), 8. See also Cheryl I. Harris, "Whiteness as Property," *Harvard Law Review* 106, no. 8 (1993): 1707–91; Eva Mackey, *Unsettled Expectations: Uncertainty, Land and Settler Decolonization* (Winnipeg: Fernwood, 2016); Aileen Moreton-Robinson, *The White Possessive: Property, Power, and Indigenous Sovereignty* (Minneapolis: University of Minnesota Press, 2015).

17. Frantz Fanon, "Why We Use Violence," in *Alienation and Freedom,* ed. Robert Young and Jean Khalfa (London: Bloomsbury, 2018), 654.

colonial regimes. Their relationships with land were invalidated, and their clearance, enclosure, and genocide were legitimated as improving the "wastelands."

Critics of Locke's justification for colonialism thus suggest that nascent systems of property and of white supremacy were mutually co-constitutive, with racial capitalism the emerging result. But, as Cedric Robinson suggests, though these racial regimes of ownership were made global through slavery and colonialism, their origins lay in the population controls familiar to Western feudal society.[18] Building on this, legal systems were written into being through the material and legal reconstruction of colonial lands as a regime of rightful possession marking distinctions between colonizer and Indigenous other.

A problem with this analysis is that the Lockean matrix obscures the fundamental role of the slave in the constitution of property regimes. Even Locke's critics foreground the central role of land, supposedly made property through colonial dispossession and the legitimizations of the labor theory. However, if we foreground the labor theory of property, the fundamental role played by ownership of chattel labor in Locke's formulations is obscured.[19] The requirement that wasted land could not be tolerated, according to Locke, did not only justify colonial expropriation but also actively required a chattel labor force.

The productive working of that land was supposedly a social good. Moreover, for Locke, the slave was "by the right of Nature, subjected to the absolute dominion and arbitrary power of their

18. Robin D. G. Kelley, "What Did Cedric Robinson Mean by Racial Capitalism?," *Boston Review,* January 12, 2017, https://bostonreview.net /articles/robin-d-g-kelley-introduction-race-capitalism-justice/.

19. Sabine Broeck, "Never Shall We Be Slaves: Locke's Treatises, Slavery, and Early European Modernity," in *Blackening Europe,* 257–70 (New York: Routledge, 2012).

masters."[20] Cultivating the wastelands through the labor of enslaved Black people was essential to produce civilized society and rational collective systems. Protection against the state of nature *as land* required the continued presence of the state of nature *as slave.*

The labor theory of property presents the positioning of slaves as chattel as derivative of property ownership through the admixture of (enslaved) labor and expropriated land. As Tapji Garba and Sara-Maria Sorentino describe, this forces the idea that the role of slavery lies primarily in working the land that the settlers have claimed. This leads to a widespread reduction of slavery to forced labor, which they call the "labor theory of slavery."[21] But here I follow Garba and Sorentino in foregrounding the ways that enslaved people also had noneconomic utility.[22] We saw in the previous chapter that the material and symbolic significance of African slavery precedes and configures global arrangements *prior* to and beyond 1492. Moreover, slavery functioned to make possible the formation of white collectives in the image of police. The continued presence of the slave is required for more than labor; the slave is required to define the contours of property ownership across the board.

For example, consider how we think about the slave as property and possession.[23] Though the logic of chattel is clear in the Barbados codes, the transformation of brutish violence into the legibility of legal form did not take the simple form of a property relation between master (as possessor) and slave (as possession).[24]

20. John Locke, *Of Political or Civil Society: The Second Treatise of Government,* with an introduction by Joseph Carrig (New York: Barnes and Noble, 2004).

21. Garba and Sorentino, "Slavery."

22. Garba and Sorentino, 786.

23. See Jared Sexton, "People-of-Color-Blindness: Notes on the Afterlife of Slavery," *Social Text* 28, no. 2 (2010): 31–56; Wilderson, *Red*; Sylvia Wynter, "1492: A New World View," in *Race, Discourse, and the Origins of the Americas,* ed. Vera Lawrence Hyatt and Rex Nettleford, 5–57 (Washington, D.C.: Smithsonian Institution Press, 1995).

24. Orlando Patterson, "On Slavery and Slave Formations," *Review of Sociology* 3 (1977): 413.

This simple form would mirror a typical understanding of the property relation as legally marking who can be excluded from ownership of certain things so that exploitation can be organized around class hierarchies. However, following Cheryl Harris's argument that property should be understood as a set of relations, we may consider how the slave codes made legal the assertion of claims to *collectively* limit and exclude access and power over things or persons.[25] That is to say, the form that the property relationship takes is primarily one of proscription and limit across relationships between groups of people and things that are thereby consolidated in the process.

Considering property as foremost a mode of social organization clarifies how it operates as a technology of domination.[26] Though this view is prima facie coherent with the labor theory, by focusing on how Black slaves were integral to the emerging property relation, we can better see how liberal property regimes were inextricable from collective subjection. For example, the metaphorical slave that so animated colonial modernity provided an example of negative freedom against which to ground autonomy. Across the Enlightenment period, slavery became forged into a specter against which a multitude of injustices could be named—from unjust taxation to state or church control.[27] Slavery was therefore abstracted away from the anti-Black violences of the plantation and remade as universal oppression or obstacle to the making of autonomy and self-possession. In these debates, slavery, as Sabine Brock writes, "actually de-signified black social death in New World regimes of enslavement."[28]

25. Harris, "Whiteness." See also Kevin Gray, who claims that "'property' is the name given to a legally (because socially) endorsed constellation of power over things and resources. Property is not a thing at all, but a socially approved power-relationship in respect of socially valued assets." Gray, "Equitable Property," *Current Legal Problems* 47 (1994): 160.

26. Nichols, *Theft,* 130.

27. See Broeck, "Never."

28. Broeck.

This metaphorical slavery therefore necessarily disavowed a slavery that cannot possibly be inhabited by those whose freedoms are won in distinction with it. The identification of Africa with slavery, as Binder points out, "suggest[s] that freedom was in large measure identified by . . . whites as freedom from the black race."[29] We see in the Barbados codes the making legible of a framework of relative freedoms against the Black slave. Unlike those who could potentially be freed from metaphorical slavery (and indentured servitude), Rinaldo Walcott describes how the slave, and any child of matrilineal descent, could not possibly be free because he was by his nature destined to remain under domination in violence.[30] Black enslaved people had no autonomy or capacity to act freely because that was invested only in their white masters.[31]

The sedimenting of Black people as chattel slaves into law was inextricable from the making of white property regimes, where this was primarily understood as a means of consolidating the rights of white people. Sabine Broeck discusses this at length, explaining how slaves functioned to signify the *right to property* for white people.[32] The expansion and distribution of property regimes and mastery over slaves had vastly enlarged the experience of entitlements for white people. As Broeck suggests, this allowed the power of knowing the world for oneself to become more widespread, while also allowing for a central distinction to be made between those who possessed property and those who were themselves possessed.[33]

By virtue of their inclusion in collective mastery, even white indentured servants were granted the possibility of freedom even while under contract. Freedoms lay along a continuum between plantation owner (master) and indentured servant (unfree laborer

29. Binder, "Slavery," 2100–2101.

30. Rinaldo Walcott, *On Property: Policing, Prisons, and the Call for Abolition* (Windsor, Ont.: Biblioasis, 2021), 7.

31. Patterson, "On Slavery," 39.

32. Broeck, "Never," 244.

33. Broeck, 239.

and metaphorical slave). In distinction, the Black slave cannot appear along this continuum but rather functioned to render freedom possible *at all* insofar as their subjection provides the infrastructure for that collective mastery and possession. The legal and material practices defining collective possession over slaves functioned to enable the accumulation of rights and capacities for all whites.[34] The function played by the Black slave would therefore also shore up freedom as the potential for limits and proscription under policing and property rights codified under law. As a relationship of power, property was consolidated against and through the status of the slave.

Distinctions between servant and slave, white and Black, were made possible through the limitation and proscriptive force of property relations *as* regime of collective possession and authority. Whereas the labor theory requires that slaves as property be derivative of land-as-property, instead I am suggesting that the continual presence of the slave was required to make possible the distinctions through which property regimes could be born. The status of the slave was not derived from ownership, labor, or economy so much as that status allowed for whiteness to be set as their boundaries.[35] The slave labors, Sorentino writes,

> not only in the production of commodities, not only as a commodity, but in the further circulation of labor-power, insofar as the slave regulates between nonwaged work and wage labor, past and present, nature and history, the concrete and abstract, force and form, nothingness and species-being.[36]

34. E.g., Wilderson draws attention to the argument made by David Eltis that it was inconceivable that "prisoners of war, or vagrants—could have been converted into chattel slaves. The barrier to European slaves in the Americas lay not only beyond shipping and enslavement costs but beyond any strictly economic sphere." Eltis, "Europeans and the Rise and Fall of African Slavery in the Americas: An Interpretation," *American Historical Review* 98, no. 5 (1993): 1399–1423.

35. Marriott, *Whither*, 143.

36. Sorentino, "Abstract," 32.

Positioning slaves as property—so thinking of slaves as chattel under collective white control—was central to the coalescing of white community. To be part of civil society—which is also to be part of the regime of property—was to be distinct from slaves.[37]

The epigraph to this chapter excerpted from the codes makes explicit the tensions at the heart of this maneuver. Black people were inscribed in law as brutish and dangerous, but as chattel, they required entanglement within a system of property ensuring that they were protected "as wee doo many other goods and Chattles." The Slave, who is but a "chattel" on all *other* occasions, wrote the abolitionist William Goodell in 1853,

> becomes "a *person*" whenever he is to be *punished*! He is the only being in the universe to whom is denied all self-direction and free agency, but who is, nevertheless, held responsible for his conduct. . . . He is under the *control* of law, though *unprotected* by law and can know law only as an enemy, and not as a friend.[38]

Locke argued that those in the state of slavery are "not capable of any property, cannot in that state be considered as any part of civil society, the chief end whereof is the preservation of property."[39] The tension between the drive toward the annihilation of the state of nature and the necessary dependence of that drive on the labor of the slave is acute.

For example, Locke, having cowritten the slaveholder's Constitution of the Carolinas, ensured that liberalism would enshrine how "everything a free man does to safeguard and accumu-

37. Broeck, "Never," 239.

38. William Goodell, *The American Slave Code in Theory and Practice: Its Distinctive Features Shown by Its Statutes, Judicial Decisions and Illustrative Facts* (New York: American Anti-Slavery Society, 1858), 125.

39. Locke, *Political.* See also Roy W. Copeland, "In the Beginning: Origins of African American Real Property Ownership in the United States," *Journal of Black Studies* 44, no. 6 (2013): 646–64.

late his private property is legitimate, provided he does not encroach on another free man's property."[40] Rights over slaves were interwoven with proscription from arbitrary incursions on the domain over which those rights hold. Protection of property was thus strengthened in opposition to the arbitrary disorder of the state of nature. But, made to embody this disordering threat, the slave was both subject to property rights and the object of forcible exclusion against incursion on those rights. Where land could be "rescued" from the wasted state of nature through clearance, genocide, and labor, the slave represented a state of nature that was both irredeemable and essential to the liberal project.

Civil society was constructed through those who cannot also be part of civil society—because slaves do not have the possibility of owning themselves, by definition, they cannot take up a position within the civil society that is reliant on them. The "right rule of reason and order" in the epigraph indicates the nascent systems of civil order and liberalism in which that tension would be managed by equating order with the embedding of fundamental violences into the structure of property law.

Colonial property regimes were predicated on a system in which, as described in the previous chapter, all white people were conscripted to uphold authority of white possession over Black people, regardless of whether they owned slaves themselves.[41] The slave codes were not passed only so that planters could better control their slaves; rather, they ensured that slaves across the colonies would be controlled to uphold the property regime as a whole. Positioning the slave as chattel in law was part of the transformation of slavery into the collective condition of being for liberalism that would ensure its continuation long after slavery had been written out of law altogether.

40. Broeck, "Never," 243.
41. Walcott, *On Property,* 11.

For example, the later Slave Trade Act 1807 (officially called *An Act for the Abolition of the Slave Trade*) made it illegal for subjects of the British Crown to buy or sell slaves and be otherwise involved in the slave trade. However, the ends of slavery stuttered and staggered across the nineteenth century. Slave trading continued long after the 1807 act, and emancipation wasn't carried through by the British until the Slavery Abolition Act of 1833 was rolled into motion a year later. Even then, emancipation would apply only in the Caribbean, with the United States actively supporting slaveholding until after the American Civil War, and in many places under indirect British rule, such as Nigeria, slavery was quietly permitted into the middle of the twentieth century.

Through emancipation, supposed freedom was brought together with the strengthening of slave patrols transformed into institutionalized police forces and pervasive forms of social control, both legislative and extrajudicial.[42] Compensation for masters, apprenticeships, and control of movement coalesced into a socioeconomic exchange between master and state, rather than master and slave, operating to (re)constitute the social realm.[43] In effect, Black people were sold to the state as existing under the ward of civil society, so requiring the ongoing dispersal of subjection. Perhaps unsurprisingly, the visions of white community, property, and freedom shaped across the "new world" were, far from being destabilized in the process, embedded further. In the context of Barbados, Bruce Taylor writes of this period that the planter class experienced very little economic or social change.[44]

Colonial society—as white community and property relation— was strengthened insofar as it was made synonymous with the

42. Anthony D. Phillips, "Emancipation Betrayed: Social Control Legislation in the British Caribbean (with Special Reference to Barbados), 1834–1876—Freedom: Beyond the United States," *Chicago-Kent Law Review* 70 (1995): 1349.

43. Taija Mars McDougall, "Blackness, Terminable and Interminable" (PhD diss., University of California, Irvine, 2022).

44. Taylor, "Black," 183.

social good. As early as 1676, in response to an attempted slave rebellion, an act further restricting slave movement, punishment, and activities had been explicitly motivated by the positioning of rebellion as an assault on whites and white property.[45] This was further ingrained through emancipation, apprenticeships, and the protection of the labor force. Stability for the political community was made possible insofar as Black people became distributed property. Labor would come to be seen as a common resource for the entire community that should be guided by the interests of the plantation.[46] Sovereignty over labor did not lie with the workers but with the colonial state and plantocracy, who were therefore charged with protecting slaves from themselves.[47]

The foremost concern of the property relation has been the distribution of an interwoven relationship between possession and authority. More basic than the singular relationship between possessor and commodity is the ability to distinguish between possessor and possessed, from which other property relations follow. The thought here is that property as written into law and code—including that of the slave—was itself constructed *through* the violences of enslavement. So, as Orlando Patterson describes, the legal and social concept of ownership requires explanation in terms of slavery, rather than the other way around.[48] The consolidation of white communities as a system of exclusion and power under property law was not enabled only by specific forms of colonial violence—enabling violences had already been built in to the form of possession itself.

45. Jerome S. Handler, "Slave Revolts and Conspiracies in Seventeenth-Century Barbados," *Nieuwe West-Indische Gids/New West Indian Guide* 56, no. 1/2 (1982): 17.

46. Robert Steinfeld, *The Invention of Free Labor* (Chapel Hill: University of North Carolina Press, 1991).

47. Harris, "Whiteness," 96.

48. Patterson, "On Slavery," 38.

It is a mainstream position to consider slavery as regressive and antagonistic to capitalist development, even if it may have been a central condition of its possibility.[49] Slavery, on this view, could be understood as an anomaly in the processual formation of capitalism with the imposition of its social categories coming undone as it developed. The resurgent interest in racial capitalism has invigorated concern in how these categories may be, in fact, fundamental to the operations of capital primarily by destabilizing its supposed European origin. This, however, does little to disrupt the underlying understanding that capitalism functions through the "tendency toward universalizing wage-labor."[50] Capitalism is still understood to establish a primary relationship between capital and wage labor, and so even if slavery was essential to capitalist development, it is necessarily its exterior.

In Eric Williams's account, for example, slavery as matrix of primitive accumulation constituted the infrastructure and wealth required for industrial capitalism to take hold in Europe.[51] However, Williams reinforces a strong distinction between a regressive slavery and an ultimately liberating capitalism that proletarianized slaves through emancipation.[52] Capitalism is then understood to correspond to the end of the violences of slavery either as coherent with emancipation or as producing it. This is consistent with

---

49. See, e.g., Robert Brenner, "The Origins of Capitalist Development: A Critique of Neo-Smithian Marxism," *New Left Review*, no. 104 (1977): 25–92; Ellen Meiskins Wood, *The Origin of Capitalism: A Longer View* (London: Verso Books, 2002).

50. Sorentino, "Abstract," 22.

51. Eric Williams, *Capitalism and Slavery* (Chapel Hill: University of North Carolina Press, 1994).

52. See Robin Blackburn, *The Making of New World Slavery* (London: Verso Books, 1997); Sidney Mintz, *Sweetness and Power: The Place of Sugar in Modern History* (Harmondsworth, U.K.: Penguin Books, 1985); Guy Emerson Mount, "Capitalism and Slavery: Reflections on the Williams Thesis," *Black Perspectives*, November 21, 2015, https://www.aaihs.org/capitalism -and-slavery-reflections-on-the-williams-thesis/; Charles Post, "Capitalist Slavery in the Great Caribbean?," *Almanack*, no. 19 (2018): 321–30.

abolitionist arguments at the time that suggested emancipation would bring Black people under contract and therefore into civil society. The suggestion was that class interests would be consolidated through emancipation, which therefore brings with it a truth about labor.[53] But, as Jason Read writes, "primitive accumulation was not just a violent transformation—the violent birth throes of the rise of the capitalist mode of production—but was itself a transformation of the form of violence."[54] This mirrors the discussion in the previous chapter regarding the absorption of the slave into legal frameworks as making way for the internalization and dispersal of violence through law and norm. In the same sense, shifts toward a liberal form of capitalism operated as a transformation of the *form* of slavery.

The continuation of slavery by other means was necessary because, as we have seen, colonial modernity formed a system of dependency of Europe on Black, Indigenous, and colonized people. Emancipation caused a crisis of capital, as Walcott writes,[55] which brought about the transformation of property regimes to embed relations of power across the colonies. So, for example, the slave appeared on the ledger of property laws that protected value. Emancipation saw compensation granted to the plantocracy while the formerly enslaved were drawn into postslavery colonial rule. In August 1834, the Abolition Act provided planters with the labor force of the previously enslaved as apprentices. Though widely resisted, slaves in British colonies were supposed to serve as unpaid apprentices for up to seven years on the plantation with just one day a week to work for themselves. As Beckles writes, the planters knew

---

53. I discuss this further in the following chapter.

54. Jason Read, *The Micro-politics of Capital: Marx and the Prehistory of the Present* (Albany: SUNY Press, 2003), 84, discussed in Sorentino, "Abstract."

55. Walcott, *Long,* 36. See also Kathleen Mary Butler, *The Economics of Emancipation: Jamaica and Barbados, 1823–1843* (Chapel Hill: University of North Carolina Press, 1995).

that control over apprentices would ensure that labor continued to operate in the interests of the plantocracy.[56]

This was a unilateral dependency on land, lives, labor, and resources, reliant on the perpetuation of violence toward, and expropriation from, colonized and enslaved people. Long after abolition, Britain continued to profit directly from enslavement, evading laws by fitting out the holds of slave ships just off-coast, using Spanish or Portuguese flags, and selling confiscated slaves to slavers. Indirectly, British industry continued to depend on slave labor for cheap cotton and sugar from northern America, Cuba, and Brazil, where slavery continued until later in the nineteenth century. For example, in the 1840s, 20 percent of British sugar imports came from Cuba, where British merchants lived and helped to finance the trade. Moreover, forced labor continued across the British Empire up until the formal successes of decolonization were transfigured into other forms of imperial control.

The tensions that arose from intimacy with and dependence on those whose lives and labor Europe expropriated were central to the drive to filter, regulate, and limit access to property but also to continually subsidize through property regimes. Imperial revenues had enabled the consolidation of power for Britons as a "racial subsidy" to the metropole lasting long after decolonization. For example, unequal exchange and a superexploited postcolonial workforce allowed the white working classes within the metropole access to consumer goods, a welfare state, and a greater standard of living.[57] The logics of the plantation continued in sustained dependence on those who, while required to provide the resources for white accumulation and expropriation, are simultaneously produced as abject and incapable of property or civil society.

56. Hilary Beckles, *A History of Barbados* (Cambridge: Cambridge University Press, 2006), 95.

57. United Coloured People's Association, cited in J. Narayan, "British Black Power: The Anti-imperialism of Political Blackness and the Problem of Nativist Socialism," *Sociological Review* 67, no. 5 (2019): 957.

These plantation logics and subsidies are ongoing. With postcolonial migration into the metropole in the mid-twentieth century, an informal color bar separated people into jobs with artificially lowered wages through which superexploitation could continue inside the British state.[58] White British workers were able to leave lower-paid jobs or to supervise migrants for higher wages. Labor stratifications made possible *internal* unequal exchange, transferring surplus to subsidize labor and capital for the burgeoning white middle classes.[59] The accumulation of capital for the establishing middle classes brought about the freedoms of property ownership through and as policing and proscription from access to British wealth. For instance, in the 1960s and 1970s, white residents had abandoned inner-city areas, leading to neighborhoods becoming populated primarily by migrants of color, while the white middle class self-segregated to monocultural suburbs. This so-called white flight led to a desire to guard these white territories against what the politician Enoch Powell had named a "separate and strange population."

Central to this process were "soft" community policing projects, including seemingly innocuous projects like Neighborhood Watch. Emerging from strategies used in Northern Ireland and white communities' response to civil rights in the United States, Neighborhood Watch implicated many into routine and formalized low-level intelligence gathering. The seemingly antagonistic

58. A. Sivanandan, "From Resistance to Rebellion: Asian and Afro-Caribbean Struggles in Britain," *Race and Class* 23, no. 2–3 (1981): 112.

59. Arghiri Emmanuel, *Unequal Exchange: A Study of the Imperialism of Trade* (New York: Monthly Review Press, 1972). The framework of super-exploitation here calls attention to the nonuniformity of labor value, suggesting that labor time and economic value are nonlinear where the value of labor is set under conditions of unequal exchange. For the superexploited, wages are set below the value of labor power because of a differential ability to enforce the rule of exchange. See John Smith, *Imperialism in the Twenty-First Century: Globalization, Super-exploitation, and Capitalism's Final Crisis* (New York: Monthly Review Press, 2016).

drives toward individual acquisition and collective action were made interdependent in service of marshaling differential power over space, property, and the means of accumulation. The suburbs needed their middle-class self-defense leagues to embed surveillance into everyday life and continue to draw distinctions and limits within and between communities.[60]

The protection and exclusion at work in schemes like Neighborhood Watch were part and parcel of a conscription to uphold the authority of white possession against those people deemed both irredeemable and essential. The formation of collective blocs like neighborhood associations and white-only labor unions was fundamental not only to the protection from and exclusion of Black people but also to the continuation of subsidies of white possession at the cost of being conscripted into its policing. This collective governance produced postemancipation debt, segregation, super-exploitation, hierarchy of labor, and unequal exchange. The differences between the Black worker and the abstract worker produced under capitalism are the continued effect of "historically specific accumulation of interlocking exclusions."[61]

Just as Black presence had been required for the formation of civil society, Black people are continually demanded by global capital accumulation. Black people—recalling the slave—are made to embody tensions at the heart of property, through their exploited and predatory inclusion in property regimes, while prerequisite for their creation and the accumulation of value through them.[62] For instance, mass-scale development projects in British urban areas were set

60. Christopher Moores, "Thatcher's Troops? Neighbourhood Watch Schemes and the Search for 'Ordinary' Thatcherism in 1980s Britain," *Contemporary British History* 31, no. 2 (2017): 230–55.

61. Sorentino, "Abstract," 32.

62. Keeanga-Yamahtta Taylor, *Race for Profit: How Banks and the Real Estate Industry Undermined Black Homeownership* (Chapel Hill: University of North Carolina Press, 2021).

in motion in the late 1990s under the rubric of urban renewal. The "sink estate" was at the center of these plans—essentially a translation of the ghetto—and formulated as a space beyond salvation. This would open up inner-city housing to wealthier renters but also to the mass accumulation of wealth through public–private partnerships like private finance initiatives. The conditions of possibility for the discourse and demolition of sink estates were disinvestment, state attrition, and infrastructural negligence. The underlying logic supporting these violences was the economic and social differentiation of spaces into places for neglect, exploitation, and disposal.[63]

But with these revanchist policies of urban "development," the accumulation of capital has become increasingly reliant on the intensification of separation—of precarious bedsits, multiplying rents, and luxury flats both proximate and separated. The sink estate becomes not only the site for urban renewal but also the site of violence and fear. For example, in 2016, Conservative prime minister David Cameron wrote,

> Step outside in the worst estates, and you're confronted by concrete slabs dropped from on high, brutal high-rise towers and dark alleyways that are a gift to criminals and drug dealers. The police often talk about the importance of designing out crime, but these estates actually designed it in. Decades of neglect have led to gangs, ghettos and anti-social behavior.[64]

These areas were framed as "breeding grounds" for social unrest, for terrorism, for gang violence. Black criminality was made contagious in these discourses, requiring not only quarantine to the sink estate but far more invasive management of their inhabitants. Because gangs had supposedly rendered them "no-go areas," according to work and pensions secretary Iain Duncan Smith, the sink estate

63. Lowe, *Intimacies,* 150.
64. David Cameron, "Estate Regeneration," *Sunday Times,* January 10, 2016, https://www.gov.uk/government/speeches/estate-regeneration-article-by-david-cameron.

required the cleansing demolition of private development to quell the possibility of a disintegrating nation-state.

However, redevelopment does not only push people out of areas. The separation of high-wage tech, information, and management work from a low-wage service sector has the effect of tightly coupling both together. As lockdowns under COVID-19 confirmed, the wealthy are reliant on service workers, cleaners, child minders, and food delivery riders, who are required to live elsewhere and hidden from view.[65]

Within this spatialized intimacy, policing forms a tissue of intimate segregations. Corporate–state collaborations operate to ensure that access and movements are tightly controlled, with targeted policing used alongside schemes like Met Patrol Plus, which would increase the police force within an area by allowing businesses and local authorities to match-fund policing in a "two-for-one" deal. Regulating the lives of the Black urban poor has become a primary activity for police and property. Where developments fail to trigger loopholes to evade building a small number of affordable homes, separate entrances are often created. These "poor doors" preclude access to those residents from building amenities like gardens, gyms, and play areas. In conjunction with a massive private security industry, spaces of "regeneration" consolidate partnerships between local authorities, policing, and private companies.

Building on community policing strategies, a barrage of antisocial behavior order powers allow for increasing control of people's movement. For instance, dispersal orders are used to bar access to specific areas on the shakiest of grounds. The criminalization of people is supported by a routine military-style presence, raids, and mass arrests, while working with public sector partners to seek injunctions and containment measures, such as checkpoints, curfews, and the removal of driver's licenses. What has resulted is

---

65. "Land and Liberty," *Research and Destroy* (blog), April 15, 2014, https://researchanddestroy.wordpress.com/2014/04/15/land-and-liberty/.

a distributed and decentralized mode of policing at the nexus of capital, politics, and security working not only to confine and territorialize people but to manage the tensions of proximity through illusions of separation.[66]

Although the plantation has become widely recognized as the site of policing's emergence and consolidation, policing is most often characterized as the thin blue line of property protection. This relies on an articulation of property regimes in which land and commodity born through violent dispossession and colonial law are to be protected from incursion by racialized people.

Here I have suggested instead that the Lockean account underlying this sort of approach leads us away from the tensions at the heart of property *as* plantation. The machinery through which civil society was created required the institution of property through the dispersal of subjection. Whiteness was formed through collective subjection *as* collective possession. Liberal capitalism is required to manage the tensions of a social order demanding the presence of Black people while being barred from taking up a position within it. These tensions, rooted in property's aporetic form *as* the plantation, continue to drive deployments of violence required for expropriation and global accumulation through predatory inclusion.

The machinery of capitalism has operated to generalize and entrench property relations as a collective web of relations in which terror is ratified by and submerged under legal rights. This runs against the grain of seeing police as involved primarily in protecting property. This isn't incorrect so much as it is misleading. Rather, property itself is primarily a relationship of policing, protection, and proscription. Property and police coincide—which is to say, property is police.

66. Cedric Parizot, "Temporalities and Perceptions of the Separation between Israelis and Palestinians," *Bulletin du Centre de recherche français à Jérusalem* 20 (2009).

3. The Police Are the Reform

After the freeing of slaves came lynching campaigns, segregation, ghettoization, discrimination, and now police wars and vicious imprisonments. After belated and half-hearted federal attempts at ameliorative programs in the 1960s and 1970s, Black people in this country still die younger, make less money, suffer poor housing, inferior community services, low educational attainments, tremendous police brutality, and, of course, the everyday injuries of race.

—HAUNANI KAY TRASK

LET ME RETURN to the words with which I began—to let the phrase "the future remain the same" echo and reverberate. This chapter builds on earlier suggestions that law and police were part and parcel of a program of reform from the start. First, I emphasize how postemancipation and colonial logics of the benevolent civilizer have been reproduced in continuity with contemporary social-liberal explanations of "crime" or violence. Kant and Hegel's approach to race and civilization is central to understanding the legitimation of the infinite postponement of emancipation, which upheld movements for abolition that reformed slavery and deferred freedoms.[1]

In this light, rather than focusing on modernity's racialized temporalities, or arguing that the chronopolitical exclusion of Black people promotes a future as white destiny, I show how the irrevocability of Blackness indexes a fissure within modernity's teleology.

1. But see also Walcott, *Long*.

I suggest that the conjunction *police-reform* indexes a specific mode of history, in which history's (a)sequentiality relies on both the inescapably regressive status of Black people and their eventual annihilation. The problem of modernity is not a white destiny that excludes all others—it is that white destiny is both necessary and impossible. The universality of anti-Black policing forms both the unthinkable ground of modernity's futurity and its irredeemable failure to petition the new.

The 1999 Macpherson report was perhaps the most significant call for police reform in recent British history. The prior investigation of the police response to the 1993 murder of Stephen Lawrence found the Metropolitan Police to be institutionally racist. The finding seemingly represented a significant shift from the Scarman Report of nearly two decades earlier that investigated the 1981 Brixton uprising. Lord Scarman had pitched the blame for "tensions" between Black communities and the police at perceptions of institutional racism and the nature of Black family structures, while conceding that there were a few bad apples within the police force. Scarman spoke of "understandable" failures of Black communities to deal with oppression and poverty, suggesting that unemployment and family structure lay at the root of the uprising.[2]

In contrast, Macpherson argued for action to be taken across police and social agencies. The report called for seventy reforms to policing and criminal law as well as suggestions for reforming local government, the National Health Service, and the school system. At the time, the report was widely decried by stakeholders in white supremacy, but over time—and particularly at points where the compact is again at risk—those reforms are said to have been

2. See Evan Smith, "Unravelling the Thatcherite Narrative: The 1981 Riots and Thatcher's 'Crisis Years,'" *New Historical Express* (blog), 2013, https://hatfulofhistory.wordpress.com/2013/01/09/unravelling-the -thatcherite-narrative-the-1981-riots-and-thatchers-crisis-years/.

embedded into a transformed police force. In 2020, for instance, Metropolitan police chief Cressida Dick stated that the police had embraced Macpherson's challenge:

> I was the person charged with implementing the recommendations and I'm very proud of what we did. I think we've come a very, very, very long way.[3]

The repetition here—very, very, very—indicates both movement and punctuation. Social progress is tied to a dialectical relationship between police as institution and the progressive social movements from which oppositions to specific instances of policing arise. The temporalities of progress and reform are compressed as if an incantation that would confine anti-Black policing to the past.

Even aside from the arguments made in previous chapters, social pressures on policing cannot be simplistically indexed either to historically contingent societal norms or to relatively universal structures of law and civil order. Moreover, as critics have long argued, reforms embedded into policing operate as part of a machinery of deferral through which progress can be produced and measured within the frameworks of liberalism.[4]

But this suggests a more deeply embedded problem. Resistance to police is dealt with insofar as reforms are the process through which oppositions to police can be internalized and policing remade. Reforms are counted as progressive insofar as they are also the stasis of return to and "making good" with the anti-Black state. Calls for reform embed a promise of progress into a political time that will never arrive.

As such, *police-reform* can be considered a conjunction that not only defines and delimits police opposition with consequences that

3. Imogen Braddick, "Met Is Not Institutionally Racist, Says Commissioner Cressida Dick," *Evening Standard,* August 13, 2020, https://www.standard.co.uk/news/crime/cressida-dick-met-not-institutionally-racist-a4524421.html.

4. Savannah Shange, *Progressive Dystopia: Abolition, AntiBlackness, and Schooling in San Francisco* (Durham, N.C.: Duke University Press, 2019), 4.

ensure the deferral of progress by oscillating around stasis and progress but also encapsulates a fundamental temporal operation of colonial modernity that thrives on anti-Black violence as its condition.

It is often supposed that history was brought into being through colonial modernity insofar as linear temporality was produced through its categories.[5] Thus a sequential form of temporal order—of progression, development, and expansion—was set *against* the state of nature (embodied by Black African people) and *toward* a future determined by (European) man.[6] Blackness is both necessary to and also positioned outside of time—as anachronistic and subject to nature's caprice.[7] Concepts of backwardness and pastness provided a framework that justified colonialism as part of the process of evolution toward modernity, as Walter Johnson writes.[8] The sequentiality produced ensures that Black African people would perpetually be in a position of "catching up" to white time or consigned to a regressive past. The myth accepted by both critics and advocates of imperialism as civilizing mission is, therefore, that the force of imperial conquest imposed backwardness on the colonized.

For instance, Kant's cosmopolitanism has usually been understood as a kind of gradual perfectibility in which the goal of history lies with the global ordering of humanity under universal principles of law and morality. Hegel also judged that history proper begins only with the Caucasian race.[9] The blame is placed with a

5. Mills, "Chronopolitics"; Hesse, "Racialized."

6. Mignolo, *Darker,* 151.

7. Michael Hanchard, "Afro-modernity: Temporality, Politics, and the African Diaspora," *Public Culture* 11, no. 1 (1999): 245–68.

8. Walter Johnson, "Possible Pasts: Some Speculations on Time, Temporality and the History of Atlantic Slavery," *American Studies* 45, no. 4 (2000): 485.

9. Robert Bernasconi, "With What Must the Philosophy of World History Begin? On the Racial Basis of Hegel's Eurocentrism," *Nineteenth Century Contexts* 22 (2000): 183–84.

supposed incapacity of Black Africans to determine a universal order from nature, which causes their enslavement to arbitrariness.[10] Humanity is here defined through the cultural achievement of history. Hegel writes that "what we properly understand by Africa, is the Unhistorical, Undeveloped Spirit, still involved in the condition of mere nature."

Hegel shares Kant's insistence that rational law is the basis of freedom requiring the subordination of naturalness to order-as-progress. For Hegel, Black Africans are bound to their senses and so incapable of the negation of the given that would be required to distance themselves from nature and become part of history. They are entrapped within immediacy. So, to paraphrase Zakkiyah Iman Jackson, Hegel formulates a conception of "the African" that is of time but not in time.

The binding of the political remaking of the world within the present is possible on condition of future novelty. It is important to foreground that the future cannot merely be a given but must be constructed, because futurity is not by itself necessarily novel. Change occurring through contingency and chance must therefore be subordinated to *progress* that is built through the actions of human reason. Any supposed "civilizing mission" of imperial expansion must then re-form the earth through culture in accord with reason and law, so recursively embedding the global development of history. In Kant's later work, the actions of reason are thereby understood as a constructive project that turns the material of the earth into the world. As Kant writes, "without man all of creation would be a wasteland, gratuitous and without final purpose."[11] This project is teleological. Growth from a "lawless state of savagery" is intertwined with a developmental theory of natural order that promises the remaking of the earth in the image of a Europe to come.

10. See Jackson, *Becoming*.

11. Immanuel Kant, *Opus Postumum* (Cambridge: Cambridge University Press, 1993); Bennington, *Kant*, 153.

In this light, Robert Louden suggests that Kant is committed to all humans eventually sharing a common destiny.[12] For example, Kant writes that "the oriental nations would never improve themselves on their own," that "all peoples on earth . . . will gradually come to participate in progress," and that "we must search for the continual progress of the human race in the Occident and from there spreading around the world."[13] But this global ordering of humanity is to be enforceable under violence against any society not yet deemed to have escaped the "lawless state of nature."[14]

This prepared the path for Hegel's dialectical movement through history toward freedom understood as a correlation between the rational human mind and the institutions that humans create.[15] Building on Kant's concern with policing self-interest to support the a priority of reason, Hegel is concerned to see how history and culture set in motion the process of reason's self-realization in the world. World history is constituted through the integration and absorption of alterity through a process of negation and overcoming of prior civilizations that consolidates advanced forms of culture. European culture emerges as a series of dispositions of reciprocal limitation and adjustment along a racialized hierarchy of perfectibility that relies on the progressive manufacture and artificialization of the earth as the world.[16] This is a generative and reciprocal relationship of *poiesis* between reason and its external scaffolds that is also reliant on a story of progression and the temporality of a world to come.[17]

12. Robert B. Louden, *Kant's Impure Ethics: From Rational Beings to Human Beings* (Oxford: Oxford University Press, 2002).

13. Kant, cited in Bernasconi, "Will."

14. Immanuel Kant, *Perpetual Peace and Other Essays* (Cambridge, Mass.: Hackett, 1983), 98.

15. M. A. R. Habib, *Hegel and Empire: From Postcolonialism to Globalism* (Berlin: Springer, 2017), 6.

16. Iain Hamilton Grant, "'At the Mountains of Madness': The Demonology of the New Earth and the Politics of Becoming," in *Deleuze and Philosophy*, ed. Keith Ansell-Pearson, 103–24 (London: Routledge, 2002).

17. See also Derrida, "Force."

As Andrea Long Chu suggests, for Hegel, world history is the dialectical process through which freedom is actualized in the form of the rational state.[18] This dialectic is inherently expansive, moving to envelop a world and, as Hegel writes, "drives a specific civil society to push beyond its own limits . . . in other lands, which are either deficient in the goods it has overproduced or else generally backward in industry."[19] This is justified, because "only certain races produce peoples,"[20] as Hegel wrote, so "one must educate the Negroes in their freedom by taming their naturalness."[21] Deracination, enslavement, and plantation work formed the basis of "education" for Hegel.

Similar logics were prevalent across postemancipation Barbados. For example, Reverend William Marshall Harte took a then controversial stance that, even given the supposedly low capacity of Black people, they could be improved through ongoing instruction, even becoming equal with their white masters.[22] This *equality-to-come* was used to preempt and tackle resistance to the criminalization of Black people. For example, refusals to allow children to be bonded by apprenticeships was quickly met with paternalistic calls to apparently help those children from a listless and immoral state. Similarly, an attempt to pay the equivalent wage that plant-

18. Andrea Long Chu, "Black Infinity: Slavery and Freedom in Hegel's Africa," *Journal of Speculative Philosophy* 32, no. 3 (2018): 416.

19. Georg W. F. Hegel, *The Philosophy of Right* (Cambridge, Mass.: Hackett, 2015), S246. See Albert O. Hirshman, "On Hegel, Imperialism, and Structural Stagnation," *Journal of Development Economics* 3 (1976): 1–8.

20. Georg W. F. Hegel, *Hegel's Philosophy of Mind*, trans. W. Wallace and A. V. Miller, rev. Michael Inwood (Oxford: Oxford University Press, 2007), 47.

21. Cited in Alison Laura Stone, "Hegel and Colonialism," *Hegel Bulletin* 41, no. 2 (2020): 247–70.

22. See J. T. Gilmore, "The Rev. William Harte and Attitudes to Slavery in Early Nineteenth-Century Barbados," *Journal of Ecclesiastical History* 30, no. 4 (1979): 461–74.

ers had previously provided in rations was justified by arguments that increased wages would make the laborers lazy and lacking in impetus to develop skills.[23]

Dawn Harris discusses how terms like "idle" and "unsettled" were used in the Apprentices Act to suggest that Black people would exist in a state of unproductive wandering without plantation oversight.[24] Punitive measures and incarceration were given credence by appeal to the improvement and protection of Black people against this idleness. Harris goes on to write of how these ideas became particularly evident in how important labor was thought to be in transforming potential criminals into law-abiding citizens.[25]

So, imprisonment was coupled with penal labor, and techniques like using treadmills in prisons encapsulated the myth of improvement through pointless labor. Similar justifications were used to motivate the policing of movement, with the guiding thought that the plantation was the central place where otherwise troublesome Black people could be made productive.[26] Restrictions on emigration, for example, were justified by humanitarian safeguarding of those requiring protection from the ignorance produced by their recent absolute dependence.[27]

The interplay of explicit violence with the violences of moralistic paternalism was particularly evident in the much later process of emancipation and attempted reconstruction on mainland North America. In the South, violent reaction against emancipation was widespread, with organizations like the Ku Klux Klan and the Redeemers operating a war of terror and frenetic order against the backdrop of radical reconstruction. As W. E. B. Du Bois discusses, this paramilitary violence, including "lynching and mob law . . . murders and cruelty," was an attempt to maintain and reassert white

---

23. Taylor, "Black," 192.
24. Harris, *Punishing*, 101.
25. Harris, 108.
26. Harris, 108.
27. Sir Charles Grey, 1842, cited in Taylor, "Black," 186.

governance.[28] This, as Du Bois suggests, was the result of a strengthening ("merging their blood so completely") of the ties between the plantocracy and the "rising poor whites."[29]

However, where this violence was obviously antagonistic to the northern movement toward freedoms, ultimately both operated to ensure that white supremacy would be maintained.[30] The violence of moralizing reform was ingrained in the white desire to rehabilitate the Black slave through the civilizing narratives that governance and control were required. So, for instance, Hartman describes how marriage, which had been previously denied (not only in contract but also in practice), became not just permitted but actively enforced as a form of social control, and through which Black men were often required to assume responsibility for the offspring of slaveholders and Black women.[31]

In this context, we can focus on how the discourse of paternalism and protection functioned to position the state, planter, and white community as "civilizer" of Black people for the good of "all."[32] Systems of apprenticeship and tied work, criminalization and continued colonialism, were justified through this discourse of racial maturity. White authority over slaves could be continued through emancipation by invoking an obligation on behalf of white people to reform and civilize Black people. As a result, as Binder details, the supposed incapacity of the slave became conjoined to the suggestion that they might become eligible for freedom only through

28. W. E. B. Du Bois, *Black Reconstruction: An Essay toward a History of the Part Which Black Folk Played in the Attempt to Reconstruct Democracy in America, 1860–1880* (New York: Harcourt Press, 1935), 54.

29. Du Bois.

30. See Herbert Shapiro, *White Violence and Black Response: From Reconstruction to Montgomery* (Amherst: University of Massachusetts Press, 1988).

31. Saidiya V. Hartman and Frank B. Wilderson III, "The Position of the Unthought," *Qui Parle* 13, no. 2 (2003): 194–95.

32. Taylor, "Black," 184.

the perpetuation of white command.[33] The burgeoning liberal emphasis on the self-sustaining individual within a free market was held together with the subordination of Black people's concern for movement and work to the "collective good."

Together with imperial expansion, transformations from slave societies to postslavery colony were saturated with this idea of the "civilizing mission." In this moment, European thought provided justifications for the continuation of subjugation and control—the general suggestion being that European enslavement, instruction, and control were vital to the future inclusion of *all* people within the unfolding story of humanity. So, inclusion under the domain of universal humanity continued core aspects of slavery in that the Black person remained under the "care" of a whiteness ordained with the determination of life and violence.[34]

Across this long history of reformist progress, endless deferrals of emancipation have further submerged the violences of policing "below the corporeal schema," to draw on Fanon.[35] Finding its culmination in Hegel, the hierarchy of perfectibility attributes universal moral properties to white Europeans, which relies on exclusions and subordination of Europe's "others." Many have argued that the so-called education and imperial support offered require the deferral of progress through a logic of endless postponement.[36]

However, in this context, we can revisit how Fanon's analysis of the Hegelian dialectic pushes beyond more standard critiques

33. Binder, "Slavery," 2072.

34. Patrice D. Douglas, "Belle's Beloved: Hauntings, Feminized Slave Ships, and the (Im)possible of Writing Black Women," talk delivered at Black Feminism beyond the Human, Duke University, 2021, https://www.youtube.com/watch?v=eKlyq3itFSM.

35. Frantz Fanon, *Black Skin, White Masks,* trans. Charles L. Markmann (London: Pluto Press, 1986), 111.

36. P. J. Brendese, *Segregated Time* (Oxford: Oxford University Press, 2023).

that center a humanity foreclosed by the European as the universal archetype of humanity.[37] The binding of the Black African into temporality cannot be processed as a chronopolitical exclusion that focuses exclusively on the endless deferrals of a continually postponed freedom.[38]

Wrenching history into being such that modernity's novelty could be unshackled from nature's contingency requires rupture from, rather than exclusion of, Blackness. The settler makes history, Fanon writes: "He is the absolute beginning, 'This land is created by us.'"[39] The impossibility of ordering the symptomatic disorder ensconced in the Black African ensures the universalization of anti-Black violence, but it also indexes colonial modernity's aporia: anti-Black violence is the necessary motor for white destiny. For example, race is irrevocable for Kant: "race, when once it has taken root and extinguished the other seeds, resists all further transformation because the character of race at one point became dominant in the generative power."[40] Any commitment to the progression of the human species cannot possibly involve Black people, who compromise Kant's understanding of human destiny.[41]

As such, the universalizing movement of liberal modernity would seem to lead inexorably toward racial genocide.[42] Indeed, as Kant put it in his notes on anthropology, the progression of *Man* tends toward an end in which "all races will be extinguished . . . only not that of the Whites."[43] The future of the world is therefore a

37. See Denise Ferreira Da Silva, *Toward a Global Idea of Race* (Minneapolis: University of Minnesota Press, 2007); Homi K. Bhabha, "'Race,' Time and the Revision of Modernity," *Oxford Literary Review* 13, no. 1 (1991): 193–219.

38. Chu, "Black," 417.

39. Fanon, *Wretched*.

40. Kant, cited in Bernasconi, "Will."

41. Bernasconi, "Will." See Kant's essay "Of the Different Races of Human Beings" (1775).

42. See John Harfouch, *Another Mind–Body Problem: A History of Racial Non-being* (Berlin: Global Academic, 2018).

43. Kant, *Anthropology*, note 1520.

White destiny grounded on the eventual wiping out of "all of the Americas."[44] Although opposed to active genocide, Kant considers it to be predetermined by nature as its "hidden plan": "not through the act of murder—that would be cruel—but they will die out."[45] For Kant, the progress of the world will ensure that it is remade as white.[46]

As sketched, for Hegel, world history is produced through the subordination and dialectical overcoming and subsequent absorption of alterity. The condemnation of Black Africans to absolute alterity and regression thus requires imperial intervention that could ensure the global advancement of civilization. However, Hegel agrees with Kant's judgment that "Negroes . . . cannot move to any culture,"[47] because their "condition is incapable of any development or culture, and their condition as we see it today is as it has always been."[48] Denied the possibility of development, Black Africans are frozen in and through time.[49]

There is a fissure within modernity's teleology. Fanon draws attention to the fact that "at the basis of Hegelian dialectic [is] an absolute reciprocity that must be highlighted."[50] The dialectical machinery of history operates through mutual recognition, with alterity moving to reinvent both past and present as a process of

44. Kant.

45. Kant, VIII, XXV. See also Flikschuh and Ypi, *Kant*; Paul Gilroy, *Against Race* (Cambridge, Mass.: Harvard University Press, 2000), 60; Charles Mills, *The Racial Contract* (Ithaca, N.Y.: Cornell University Press, 1997), 72.

46. Huaping Lu-Adler, "Kant and Slavery; or, Why He Never Became a Racial Egalitarian," *Critical Philosophy of Race* 10, no. 2 (2022): 263–94.

47. Georg W. F. Hegel, *Lectures on the Philosophy of World History*, ed. Robert F. Brown and Peter C. Hodgson (Oxford: Oxford University Press, 2019), 1:S67.

48. Georg W. F. Hegel, *Reason in History: A General Introduction to the Philosophy of History* (New York: Liberal Arts Press, 1953), S190.

49. Habib, *Hegel*, 81.

50. Fanon, *Black*, 191.

overcoming by sublation.[51] The attempted sublation of prior stages requires shared purpose and ground with the subject of a recognition because a "one-sided activity would be useless."[52] But situated in the Manichean world of plantation and colony, Fanon argues that where for "Hegel there is reciprocity; here the master laughs at the consciousness of the slave."[53]

So, considered from within Hegel's vision of history, dialectical circuity is shut down, making any "two-way movement unachievable."[54] The abrogation of history from Black people must operate by rupture such that Blackness cannot possibly be recognized. But in the process, as M. R. Habib points out, white people thereby disable themselves from entry into the recognitive process.[55] The Manichean world of mutual exclusion—of absolute oppositions that cannot be unified, neither interdependent nor interpenetrating—indexes a nondialectical antinomy that short-circuits historical progress.[56]

If modernity were to be eventually capable of achieving its asymptotic goals, it would seem to require not the dialectical progression of the entire species but the annihilation of those who were deprived of entry. However, the movement of history itself requires the irrevocably atemporal status of the Black African to serve as the Other who must be sublated such that European freedom can be realized.[57] This is to say that Hegel's dialectical machinery is aporetically reliant on the eternal suspension of the Black African

51. See Gavin Arnall, *Subterranean Fanon: An Underground Theory of Radical Change* (New York: Columbia University Press, 2020), 15ff.

52. Georg W. F. Hegel, *The Phenomenology of Spirit* (Oxford: Oxford University Press, 2018), S182.

53. Fanon, *Black,* 39.

54. Fanon, 192.

55. Habib, *Hegel,* 68.

56. In particular, see arguments made in Arnall, *Subterranean*; Marriott, *Whither.*

57. Habib, *Hegel,* 80.

as outside of history,[58] together with the supersession of that stage of history by European interaction and transformation.

As such, the logics of colonial modernity seem to require the destruction of their own conditions. Put bluntly, temporal progress would require the annihilation of those it requires as its basis for defining time.[59] Explicating Fanon's argument, Habib clarifies this point by describing how Hegel places Africa in a permanent state of nature that simultaneously deprives those supposedly later historical stages from being able to develop through dialectical interaction with former stages.[60] The problem of modernity is therefore not a white destiny that excludes all others; it is that white destiny is both necessary and impossible.

These tensions lead to an aporia that requires impossible suture. The infinite postponement of white destiny effectuates everywhere more vicious and yet more petrified violences. The "seeming infinitude of total war"[61] cannot be shifted into a domain of reciprocal relation. As Marriott writes, Blackness cannot be a possible object of knowledge—neither explicable nor experienceable by the systems through which it is produced.[62] As Marriott writes of Fanon's *n'est pas* of Blackness,

---

58. Mario Gooden, *Dark Space: Architecture, Representation, Black Identity* (New York: Columbia University Press, 2016).

59. Anna M. Agathangelou and Kyle D. Killian, eds., *Time, Temporality and Violence in International Relations: (De)Fatalizing the Present, Forging Radical Alternatives* (New York: Routledge, 2016); Mark Rifkin, *Beyond Settler Time: Temporal Sovereignty and Indigenous Self-Determination* (Durham, N.C.: Duke University Press, 2017).

60. Habib, *Hegel*, 68.

61. David Marriott, "Judging Fanon," *Rhizomes* 29, no. 1 (2016): S12. I am thinking with Felicia Denaud's incisive concept of the "unnameable war." Denaud, "At the Vanishing Point of the Word: Blackness, Imperium, and the Unnameable War" (PhD diss., Brown University, forthcoming).

62. Marriott, "Judging," S13.

the thing that Blackness is *is not*—and accordingly, our relation to it—the mark of a rupture which is both exterior and radically intimate, an abyss which is situated at the limit of judgment, thought, and desire: a monstrance without center or end.

This "*is not*" confounds both Kantian limit and Hegelian negation. As I suggested in the earlier discussion of Kant, Blackness cannot register as alterity because that would also register as a limit with attributes and referent, so allowing the machinery of dialectics to grind into motion. But because Blackness is both intimate and unassimilable—as a void that resists knowledge—dialectical movement necessarily always falters and stutters.[63]

This trajectory of thought draws attention away from dismissal or philosophical analysis of history's fissures and modernity's problems; rather, embedded within the colonial situation, their aporetic form both conditions and confounds resolution. This is to say that the tendency and drive of colonial modernity toward extinction would create "a void which empties foreign domination of its content and its object: the dominated people," as Amílcar Cabral put it. The urge to destroy the colonized would "amount to the immediate destruction of colonization," as Fanon cited of Sartre. Modernity's dependence on those it requires as its basis for defining time indexes a terminal aporia in which history is driven through the management and staving off of anti-Black genocide. What is set in motion as a project of infinite postponement is therefore not characterizable as the white paternalist or temporizing universalism in which freedoms are endlessly deferred; rather, this is an infinite postponement of the progressive political structure of the world as white destiny.

We see this dialectical machinery at work in embedding strategies of counterinsurgency into mainland British policing.[64] As explained

63. David Marriott, "Corpsing; or, The Matter of Black Life," *Cultural Critique*, no. 94 (Fall 2016).

64. I am interested in the reverberations of plantation and colonial policing to the metropole here—primarily because they remain less theorised than U.S. policing, but a similar account of the latter is in Schrader, *Badges*.

by Stuart Hall and Paul Gilroy, among others, the postcolonial im-
migrant and his family were framed as causing the extinction of
British order—making way for the reproduction of the unpolice-
ability of those seen as intrinsically antagonistic to British values.
For instance, just prior to the Brixton uprisings, on March 28, 1981,
Enoch Powell gave a speech in which he warned of the dangers of a
"racial civil war" in Britain, later echoed by the *Daily Mail*'s headline
"Black War on Police."

After the 1981 uprisings, policing models were developed that
drew directly on those used in Northern Ireland and Hong Kong.
These distilled decades of British colonial policing into command-
and-control networks, riot suppression units that were armed and
flexibly deployed, and street patrols for curfew enforcement. As
Gerry Northam writes, their

> public order tactics are a compendium of methods which have been
> tried and tested for forty years in all the former colonies. They have
> repressed dissent and put down uprisings in the Caribbean, up and
> down Africa, in the Middle East, the Indian sub-continent and in the
> Far East.[65]

In consultation with the Hong Kong police, a public order manual
was developed advising tactical options in the face of rioting that
included use of smoke, baton rounds, tear gas, and, in the case of
lethal rioting, firearms. This found justification in Lord Scarman's
report on the Brixton uprising, in which he had written that "the
police must be equipped and trained to deal with this [disorder] effectively and firmly whenever it may break out." For similar reasons,
Kenneth Newman was appointed commissioner of the Metropolitan
Police in 1982. He had previously worked for the British Palestine
Police and most recently as chief constable of the Royal Ulster
Constabulary (RUC).

The militarized policing of targeted communities had focused
attention on race and threat against the state. As Salman Rushdie

65. Gerry Northam, *Shooting in the Dark* (London: Faber and Faber,
1988), 135.

noted in the early 1980s, "for the citizens of the new, imported empire, for the colonized [Asian and Black people] of Britain, the police force represents that colonizing army, those regiments of occupation and control."[66] However, an explicit war between the state and Black and Asian communities was causing the legitimacy of the police to come under fire.

As the Institute of Race Relations had put it shortly after the 1981 uprisings, "the actions of black youth on the streets destroyed at a stroke the myth of police invincibility." In 1983, Ferdinand Mount, head of the prime minister's policy unit, wrote in the *London Evening Standard* that "the conduct of the police is being brought into question, not among parts of the working class who might regard themselves as the hereditary enemies of the constabulary, but among the respectable middle classes." Amid this, Newman recognized that it was imperative to "educate the public that the 'battle' analogy is inappropriate"—propping up policing would require the attempted sublation of violence.

Criminalization became central to this attempted sublation, developed most proximately from the strategy of "Ulsterization" in 1970s Northern Ireland (itself drawn from strategies that the United States used in Vietnam). Under the command of renowned proponent of counterinsurgency Frank Kitson, Northern Ireland saw methods of pacification and stabilization focusing on population control combined with coercive and covert murder and systematic torture that would "squeeze the Catholic population until they vomit the gunmen out of their system." Counterinsurgency, for Kitson, was a contest for legitimacy that could not be won through a military solution, "because insurgency is not primarily a military activity."

However, Bloody Sunday raised the specter of war and enemy, giving credence to the Provisional Irish Republican Army's (PIRA) framing of "civil war" with a discredited colonial army. Kitson was

66. Salman Rushdie, "The New Empire within Britain," *New Society* 9 (1982): 417–21.

removed soon afterward with a CBE (Commander of the Order of the British Empire, which is the highest-ranking award excluding knighthood/damehood), and Newman was installed to reorganize the RUC and work within a modified legal and criminal justice system. This process of Ulsterization would diffuse the remnants of enemy-centric war through the professionalization and militarization of the police, forming tactical support units and intelligence-led targeted operations. The RUC taking the primary role in policing the PIRA allowed for criminalization to transform acts of colonial war into crime scenes and PIRA members into criminals. The intent of the policy was to reconfigure political conflict as an operation against criminal gangs. As Newman later stated, the aim was to separate insurgents from community support:

> The object is to prise open and progressively widen a gap between the terrorist and the ordinary people so that they will be increasingly perceived as criminals and not as wayward political heroes.

As such, disorder was distributed across the population, making way for more complex and indirect forms of power and surveillance, with the police supposedly acting on behalf of a unified people, where that "people" also contained the enemy within. This wasn't an act of depoliticization so much as the sublation of an ongoing war against political actors with the potential to upturn existing colonial power relations.

Criminalization and professionalization thus strengthened the legitimacy of coercive force while further undermining political action against the British state by ensuring the pervasiveness of policing across people's lives. Seemingly paradoxically, the militarization of policing and the framing of threats as criminal were part and parcel of the manufacture of political consensus upholding policing by consent.

These struggles were far from disconnected to those in mainland England. With some prescience, in 1973, Conservative MP John Alec Biggs-Davison stated, "If we lose in Belfast we may have to fight in

Brixton or Birmingham. . . . Perhaps what is happening in Northern Ireland is a rehearsal for urban guerrilla war." In 2014, declassified files showed that Thatcher had also made these connections explicit in 1984, centering fears about the relationship between Catholic alienation in Northern Ireland and struggles of Black and Asian people in maintain Britain:

> If these things were done, the next question would be what comes next? Were the Sikhs in Southall to be allowed to fly their own flag?

Unsurprisingly, Newman's mainland strategy closely followed Ulsterization, with criminalization and militarization essential to transforming Black and Asian communities from enemy of the state into enemy of "the people of Britain." The enemy within would therefore become the enemy of all, because, as criminals, they would embody a struggle against social order. As Newman stated, "it would be better if we stopped talking about crime prevention and lifted the whole thing to a higher level of generality represented by the words social control."

In part, this maneuver was brought about by the "professionalization" and reorganization of policing as structure that comes to be identified with both the "people" and the domain of politics proper. New regulations instituted practices drawn from Northern Ireland across Britain, bringing social services under the banner of community policing, and a new Police and Criminal Evidence bill sought to expand powers of surveillance across public bodies. Multiagency information collection and Neighborhood Watch were integral to this reform, implicating many into routine and formalized low-level intelligence gathering that was used to justify passport raids, raids on Black clubs and meeting places, and arbitrary arrests by Special Patrol Groups.

Criminalization manufactured the normalization of this pervasive and coercive policing, with communities targeted as criminal and "constitutionally disorderly," as Newman characterized Jamaican people, now indexing not a rupture in the fabric of warfare but a break in the "normal" social order. In this way, a far more militarized police force was, by the end of Newman's tenure in 1987, granted a greater legitimacy than it had had before. The impossible limits of a total war were thereby installed and reconfigured such that violence itself is plunged into the unknowable depths of the world. The fragile dependencies of the colonial present employ practices of reform and social inclusion not as a progression but as an operation of the attempted suture of white order.[67]

Taking dependence and postponement as a spiraling point of entry into the colonial present is inimical to temporalities of succession and repositions the phrase "future remain the same."[68] This fragile setup requires the winding of violence into presence and temporal movement through which racial slavery's occult presence, as Marriott writes, is a "dead time [that] never arrives and does not stop arriving."[69] So, if "future remain the same," this is because, as Nadera Shalhoub suggests, Blackness is perpetuated death that generates the potential of life for others.[70] Indefinite postponement operates through the movement of social inclusions and exclusions in a supposedly dialectical motion as a process of management reliant on anti-Black violence.

For example, the 2021 Sewell Report chartered by the Conservative Party seemingly to appease itself (and all stakeholders in white supremacy) after antipolice protests earlier in the year similarly announced that we have reached the end of institutionalized British racism. Emerging in response to the murder of George Floyd by Minneapolis Police Department officer Derek Chauvin, British

67. Hartman, *Scenes.*

68. Hartman and Wilderson, "Position."

69. David Marriott, *Haunted Life: Visual Culture and Black Modernity* (New Brunswick, N.J.: Rutgers University Press, 2007), xxi.

70. N. Shalhoub, Roundtable on Anti-Blackness and Black-Palestinian Solidarity, Jadaliyya, June 3, 2015, https://www.jadaliyya.com/Details /32145.

protests were barely acknowledged before they were sanctioned for their violence by prime minister Boris Johnson.[71] Set in another moment of potential destabilization of the police–public compact, the report stated that incremental progress is beyond doubt, drawing attention to the relationship between progress and fatalism:

> You do not pass on the baton of progress by cleaving to a fatalistic account that insists nothing has changed.[72]

Attending to anti-Black violence operates as a fatalism in this logic— attempting to cleave stasis against progress.

Reforms are often felt as stasis and deferral. Cue the multiple reports, articles, statements analyzing progress after ten years, twenty years, forty years. These engagements often implicitly reify a notion of progressive policing, making room for reform's dialectical movement to grind into motion once more. So, in seeming opposition to Cressida Dick and the Sewell Report, a Home Affairs Committee report published in July 2021 considered the Macpherson Report twenty-two years on, bemoaning how a representative police force would not be reached at the current rate of progress for another twenty years.[73]

The oscillation continues. The 2021 Home Affairs Committee report called for reattention to Macpherson's suggested reforms and targets, centering the need for diversity within policing and the criminal justice system, and attention to stop-and-search disparities. As if in conversation with Doreen Lawrence and the Sewell Report, discussing the report, Labour MP Yvette Cooper stated,

71. BBC News, "George Floyd: Boris Johnson Urges Peaceful Struggle against Racism," June 9, 2020, https://www.bbc.co.uk/news/uk-politics -52973338.

72. Commission on Race and Ethnic Disparities, *The Report* (2020), https://www.gov.uk/government/publications/the-report-of-the -commission-on-race-and-ethnic-disparities/conclusion-and-appendices.

73. Home Affairs Committee, *The Macpherson Report: Twenty-Two Years on Home Affairs Committee* (2021), https://publications.parliament.uk /pa/cm5802/cmselect/cmhaff/139/13902.htm.

> We have found that in too many areas progress has stalled. . . . Without clear action to tackle race inequality we fear that, in 10 years' time, future committees will be hearing the very same arguments that have been rehearsed already for over 20 years.[74]

The dividing line between reform and a politics of equal-opportunity law and order is tipped out as a continuum along the binary of stall and progress. They are together productive of a state whose benevolence and viciousness are modalities of the colonial present.

The inertia and petrification of the colonial situation, which is characterized in the Sewell Report as "cleaving to a fatalistic account," is here both violence's cause and effect. The production of time as fatal (as incomplete death) operates through a fatalism (as permanent state of nature) that is both necessary and illegitimate for colonial modernity.[75] But, far from indexing stasis and fatalism, the temporality of "future remain the same" indexes a sprawling temporality that is unthinkable as temporality (or at least within temporalities marked by progress), while also providing the conditions and context for the construction of temporality as such. Thus there is no progressive possibility for Blackness in the absence of violence, just as there is no possibility for modernity to petition a future in the absence of Blackness.

Both social inclusion and exclusion operate as part of the management process of infinite postponement. The superficial antagonisms articulated in the logics of reform and progress provide the "motionless movement" in which dialectics becomes merely a "logic of equilibrium," as Hegel writes.[76] It is this dialectical ma-

74. Nadine White, "'Racism in Policing Remains an Issue, 20 Years after Macpherson Report,' Say MPs," *Independent,* July 30, 2021, https://www.independent.co.uk/news/uk/home-news/racism-policing-home-affairs-committee-b1893324.html.

75. Agathangelou and Killian, *Time.*

76. Hegel in Habib, *Hegel,* 73.

chinery that functions by moving toward the impossible suture of the colonized into a social whole.[77]

For instance, the British Conservative Party quickly capitalized on its 2021 election mandate to ramp up law-and-order politics. Just before the general election, home secretary Priti Patel said she wanted criminals to literally feel terror,[78] and leader Boris Johnson announced plans to make criminals afraid.[79] But, though many across the political spectrum painted Conservative plans as uniquely severe, at their core is a whole-society approach to tackling serious violence that has cross-parliamentary support and deep historical roots.

This is clearest with a legal duty to prevent and tackle serious violence that was originally put to consultation by then prime minister Theresa May. Building on the supposedly antiterror duty Prevent, this will require organizations like National Health Service trusts and schools to identify "warning signs" and share information about people deemed vulnerable to perpetrating serious crime.[80] The duty is backed up by discourses of violent youth radicalization from gang crime to extreme ideologies, a new Offensive Weapons Act, and Violence Reduction Units (VRUs) that integrate military, police, and civil power.

77. Glen Sean Coulthard, *Red Skin, White Masks: Rejecting the Colonial Politics of Recognition* (Minneapolis: University of Minnesota Press, 2014), 39.

78. Damian Gayle, "Home Secretary Priti Patel Criticised over Wish for Criminals 'to Feel Terror,'" *Guardian*, August 3, 2019, https://www .theguardian.com/politics/2019/aug/03/priti-patel-home-secretary-wants -criminals-to-literally-feel-terror.

79. Jacob Jarvis, "Boris Johnson Extends Stop and Search Measures to Make 'Criminals Afraid—Not the Public,'" *Evening Standard,* August 10, 2019, https://www.standard.co.uk/news/politics/boris-johnson-extends -stop-and-search-measures-to-make-criminals-afraid-not-the-public -a4210551.html.

80. Home Office, "The Serious Violence Strategy," October 21, 2019, https://www.gov.uk/government/publications/preventing-serious-violence -a-multi-agency-approach/preventing-serious-violence-summary.

Much of this is deemed acceptable by the socially liberal so long as the upstream explanations for violent crime are social exclusion and poverty rather than race and immigration status. The Public Health Approach that was advocated by the Labour Party has been promoted as a reformist model of policing that is antagonistic to the aggressive style of current Conservative discourse and policy. However, in essence, these are different management styles of the same approach, with people who represent the potential for violence requiring preemption, tagging, and risk assessment.

Discourse on "serious violence" suggests that knife crime and other street crime cannot be prevented or solved without community effort. So, ending the stabbing and killing of young (Black) people is not just the job of the police: it has passed that point and now involves the community. Yet, this community is associated with serious violence in that they are implicated. What is implied is that "the Black community" is to be blamed for not trusting the police or relying on the police too much to solve a problem not of their own making.

This requires the increasing conscription, consent, and complicity of British citizens in policing. Vital youth and community services that have been wrecked by funding cuts are to be offered grants under a new Youth Endowment Fund *provided* they work to prevent involvement in crime, are open to evaluation under violence reduction, and share their data. Shifting narratives away from a primary focus on gangs to specific group-oriented violence is being used to better aid community buy-in to violence reduction.[81] The Behavioral Change Campaign overseen by VRUs will work with successful recipients to influence behavior and generate counternarratives. This implicates and conditions community groups to reproduce the discourses and practices of their own criminaliza-

---

81. Tom Davies, Lynne Grossmith, and Paul Dawson, "Group Violence Intervention London: An Evaluation of the Shield Pilot," December 2016, https://www.london.gov.uk/sites/default/files/gvi_london_evaluation270117.pdf.

tion, while making them complicit in the idea that inner-city Black young people are at once the inevitable source of violent crime and responsible for working to undo its causes and conditions.

So, what is at stake is not merely citizens, civic officials, authorities, acting as police. The Serious Violence Duty legalizes partnerships and relationships between the police and their familial or social counterparts. Transinstitutional cooperation combines coercion with early intervention to produce precriminal spaces in which suspicion continues to be the foundation for pervasive intervention. Violence reiterated and refigured as excessive to traditional categorization of criminal offenses (immeasurable, unquantifiable) supports and maintains a duty premised on social response to a violence that is non–terror related, a social response that encompasses health, educational, and housing services. With the whole-society approach, policing doesn't simply reflect and reinforce popular morality or political aims; rather, policing actively crafts and arbitrates on people's lives, differentiating the relative viscosity and peril of movement through education systems, health care, welfare, services, employment, and communities.

Dylan Rodriguez calls our attention to *reformism* as the position that takes reform to be the primary engine of social change.[82] I have suggested analogously that the conjunction *police-reform* expresses the temporality of progress as stasis—operating as an engine through which policing can be infinitely expanded and embedded into the everyday. Reformism is the logic of supposed dialectical progress, where that process indexes the continued attempt to suture white order under police.

We have seen that the suggestion that police-reform embeds the promise of future progress through which violence may be

82. Dylan Rodriguez, "Reformism Isn't Liberation, It's Counterinsurgency," 2020, https://level.medium.com/reformism-isnt -liberation-it-s-counterinsurgency-7ea0a1ce11eb.

"solved" by remaking society to be more inclusive has a long and pernicious history. The view coheres with the now near-doctrinal identification of socioeconomic drivers for crime and violence as motivation for "improving" policing. For example, Lambros Fatsis writes of how criminologists consider poverty and inequality to be the key drivers of violence, a focus on which should be central to understanding police and crime.[83] However, both the incantation of the end of racialized policing and so-called progressive reforms further embed arrangements of violence that are endlessly re-forming.[84]

What rolls into motion with programs of social inclusion is not even a one-sided dialectic but rather a neutered dialectic whose condition is also its impossible completion. Put another way, the practice of social inclusion and exclusion is not a matter of progress but rather indexes the continuation of gratuitous violence. Any dialectical movement necessarily always falters and stutters. That is to say, the dialectical unity (whole-society) is neither only internally fractured nor a partial universal; rather, it is a struggle toward closure through the attempted making-universal of police.

The dialectical formation of whole-society is a totality whose ground is the void of anti-Black violence. Characterizing anti-Black violence as *anti*-Black violence is not a sign of negation or denotation, then, but rather must be everywhere irresolvable as the mark of white destiny's condition and impossibility. Blackness

83. Thomas Kingsley, "Criminologists Slam 'Misleading' Policy Exchange Report Linking Drill Music to Youth Violence," *Independent*, November 13, 2021, https://www.independent.co.uk/news/uk/home-news /policy-exchange-report-youth-violence-b1955691.html.

84. C. Warren, "Black Time: Slavery, Metaphysics, and the Logic of Wellness," in *The Psychic Hold of Slavery* (New Brunswick, N.J.: Rutgers University Press, 2016), 59. See also Saidiya V. Hartman, *The Time of Slavery* (Delhi: Routledge, 2012), 447–68.

relies on total war as a negation that cannot negate.[85] This is to say that the impossible yet terminal end for the project of modernity (absolute genocide) is retroactively embedded within each temporal moment such that supposed progress is constituted at the attempted suturing of future and terminus.[86] The breach that is impossible to suture continues to lend law and police its transcendental condition.

85. Marriott, "Judging," S13.

86. Bedour Alagraa, "The Interminable Catastrophe," *offshoot,* March 1, 2021, https://offshootjournal.org/the-interminable-catastrophe/.

4. The Impossibility of White Worlding

> While we can imagine emancipation from slavery as a movement across such a boundary, we can also conceive emancipation as the elimination of the boundary altogether: eliminating slavery and freedom alike.

—GUYORA BINDER

IN 2020, a fifteen-year-old Black schoolgirl from Hackney in London was strip-searched by Metropolitan police officers while menstruating. They had been called by teachers who had wrongly suspected her of carrying cannabis. As she put it, "I was held responsible for a smell, but I'm just a child."[1] For decades, this phantom aroma has enveloped Black people within the grip of stop-and-search. The violences that conspired in the traces of sillage—the olfactory signature of anti-Blackness—expose the insidiousness of policing Black working-class people in the mundane movement through the world.

We note how quickly anger at this treatment coalesced into counterinsurgency. Calling attention to law returns civil society to policing without excess, for fairness, neutrality, equality, to reify that schools are normatively safe—a space of security and care,

---

1. Jemma Crew, "Black Schoolgirl Strip Searched by Police While on Her Period—Report," *Evening Standard,* March 16, 2022, https://www .standard.co.uk/news/uk/department-for-education-metropolitan-police -services-scotland-yard-hackney-b988292.html.

as mayor of Hackney Philip Glanville suggested.[2] Security is born through policing, not only of police in schools, but of teaching staff conscripted into suspicion and report, of schooling as reproduction of discipline and hierarchy. The violences did not begin in that hostile room guarded by teachers as she was stripped and searched; those violences are originary, rooted not in transgression but in the structuring order of the world.

Abolition that targets only the institution of the police risks focusing on police brutality in the spectacularization of the mundane brutality of policing across the social world. For example, embedded within a police–citizen compact, eruptions of violence become periodically explicit through race riots, police brutality, "extrajuridical" killing, targeted and discriminatory criminalization. Where police violence oversteps this line, liberal critique attempts to suture law and police through a program of reforms that realign police and citizen along the lines of legitimate violence. The institution of the police operates at the cutting edge of policing as form of the world—operative at the threshold of its endless suture.[3]

    June 2020 saw a street party in Brixton, London, invaded by police attempts to shut down and disperse the gathering. Instead, the community forced the police out of the estate, with local residents elatedly remarking that "the police are getting run out of here."[4]

    2. Seren Hughes, "Black Schoolgirl, 15, from Hackney 'Traumatised' after Strip Search by Police While on Her Period," *My London,* March 15, 2022, https://www.mylondon.news/news/east-london-news/black -schoolgirl-15-hackney-traumatised-23400186.

    3. Steve Martinot and Jared Sexton, "The Avant-Garde of White Supremacy," *Social Identities* 9, no. 2 (2003): 169–81.

    4. Harriet Brewis and John Dunne, "Brixton Street Party Descends into Violence and Chaos with Police Car Smashed and 22 Officers Injured," *Evening Standard,* June 25, 2020, https://www.standard.co.uk/news/crime /car-smash-brixton-street-party-chaos-a4479556.html.

Police were chased away while people shouted, "Don't come round here, bro!" In the process, at least twenty-two police officers were injured, having to abandon a police car that was then broken up. Afterward, the Metropolitan Police Federation bemoaned being "met with hostility from the off." The anticipation of passivity was ingrained in the impunity of stating that "no-one expects this level of violence and hostility to just erupt at the speed it does towards police. It's horrendous. . . . It's not nice to have to go somewhere where someone wants to try and kill you."[5]

There is such joy in this hostility—in rendering this space intimidating and unapproachable for the "army of the ends," as London youth leader Yolanda Lear highlighted.[6] In these contexts, we see explicitly how actions like setting a police car alight are understood as *violence* against property. Instructively, property destruction counts as violence insofar as it is an assault on social relations, which is to say a direct assault on police not only as institution but as social relation.

We see here that in the call to disestablish the police is also the desire to foster forms of community and relation that are not over-coded by policing—that begin to articulate ways of life that destabilize the structures that are prerequisite for property regimes, dispossession, and looting community wealth. While abolition requires at the very least the disestablishment of the police, abolitionism necessarily involves also the annihilation of the colonizer, the overseer, the prison guard, border control—as structure of relation. Because of this, abolition cannot be prefigured and posi-

5. ITV, "Downing St Condemns Violence as at Least 22 Police Officers Injured at Street Party in Brixton," June 25, 2020, https://www.itv.com /news/london/2020-06-25/police-car-smashed-as-brixton-street-party -descends-into-chaos.

6. Quoted in Ed Sheridan, "Youth Worker Stopped by Police for Having His Hands in His Pockets in 'Racial Profiling' Incident," *My London*, March 12, 2021, https://www.mylondon.news/news/east-london-news /youth-worker-stopped-police-having-20115697.

tioned as political project or movement for social inclusion; rather, abolitionism requires a perpetual insurgency against the "army of the ends," against property, against civil society.

In Louisiana in 2021, a group of Black fathers gathered in the form of "dads on duty" in an attempt to preempt and prevent increasing violence among their children at a local high school. Activist and writer Harsha Walia hailed this as an example of abolition in practice.[7] However, the case is instructive in foregrounding the limitations of police abolition insofar as resistance to police can be sutured into the continuation of policing. For example, we might consider how abolition contends with violences that are pernicious and pervasive—that ensure continuing exploitation, precariousness, subsidy, and that seep into our desires and practices of community and care. How could the "dads on duty" exemplify abolition when communities are required to perform care work that does not have the capacity to undo the violences to which they are subjected? How much of this harm reduction is counterinsurgency—especially given that so much of community work is already co-opted into policing? What of the policing that comprises patriarchal and cis-heteronormative modes of interaction and control?

So, for example, where Mariame Kaba argues that "the only way to diminish police violence is to reduce contact between the public and the police," we also need to foreground the necessary operation that constantly founds publics as police. The schools in Louisiana and in Hackney are spaces of extrajudicial captivity prior to the police being called. It is through this perverse proliferation of policing everywhere and without determinable limit that we are enmeshed in worlds of subjection, security, and scrutiny. If we are not only all responsible for policing but policing is the form of the human

7. Harsha Walia (@HarshaWalia), "next time someone tells you we can't get cops out of schools," Twitter, October 23, 2021, 8:19 PM, https://twitter.com/HarshaWalia/status/1452067300484403203.

world as a permanent state of siege, then we should consider how abolitionism might not only evade the structural reassurance of white order but ensure that it is endlessly undone—to focus on how abolition might already embody the impossibility of life in this imperial world.

I want to close by considering how we might situate Fanon's consideration of invention in the context of abolitionism:

> I am not a prisoner of History. I should not seek there for the meaning of my destiny. I should constantly remind myself that the real leap consists in introducing invention into existence. In the world through which I travel, I am endlessly creating myself.[8]

To think with Fanon, let me stay with Doreen Lawrence's phrase "future remain the same," together with Marriott's analysis of this passage, which suggests that Fanon cannot be recruited into a mode of opposition or resistance to history. Developing this argument, Axelle Karera points to how Fanon's work cannot be understood through frameworks of restitution, restoration, and regeneration.[9] If abolition is indexed to the political (as project, or worlding), it is therefore always already overcoded in suturing to an impossible progress. This is to say that any *political project* of abolition *necessarily* becomes oriented toward the impossible consolidation of an order even as it attempts to overcome itself. We need to undo not only order but the possibility of ordering—the horizon of possibility that is "the world." Otherwise, as discussed in the previous chapter, fatal/ism then becomes the only possible register of resistance within the domain of the political—the idea that "future remain the same" becomes enmeshed with the injunction that progress has

8. Fanon, *Black,* 229.

9. Axelle Karera, "The Racial Epidermal Schema," in *50 Concepts for a Critical Phenomenology,* 289–94 (Evanston, Ill.: Northwestern University Press, 2019).

already been made. This means that we seek, not an end to a unitary world, but an end to worlding itself—of the impossible horizon of a unitary world.[10]

Where the idea of a world is suggestive of a unity in social totality, I have instead foregrounded the unremitting policing of multiple and intersecting relationships and interactions as its ongoing condition. This world in which everything is police is unlivable by design—it is sustained by expropriation of Black lives, land, and labor and maintained by policing embedded into its very foundation. The world cannot be sutured *as* world. If it is in the impossible constitution of the world through which categories of human, property, and freedom are constructed, any project through which they would be restored is necessarily a practice of reassurance of that world (which is to say, its policing).

The infinite postponement of anti-Black genocide effectuates everywhere more vicious and yet more petrified violences. As this plantation world tends toward annihilation and antagonism, life support systems operate at the tip of a balancing act between an unlivable world and the machinery of earth's ruin. If incomplete death is the *ongoing* condition of possibility for white life, then the violence productive of Blackness is necessarily perpetual. The white world that incomplete death makes possible cannot be fully realized. This foundational dependence both undermines and underpins the drive toward a coherent white social order. With Fanon and Doreen Lawrence, the supposed closure of colonial modernity against those "outside" is its ongoing yet impossible condition.

Though the legislative architecture of colonial order preemptively attempts to dissolve alterity, it was born of contact with the ungraspable, the unorderable, the unspeakable, as that which must be policed as threat to it. Against the impossible suture of the world, I have foregrounded policing across that which is both within and without. This antinomy points toward the realization

---

10. See also Palmer, "Otherwise."

that the world is impossible—which is to say that capture, control, preemptive annihilation, are not completable projects but require the continued operations of breach and suture. The necessary inclusion of Blackness into colonial modernity reveals that Blackness is produced primarily as protective system for the modern human (i.e., whiteness) whose realization is thereby rendered impossible. (Anti)Blackness is both the condition of the world and also what puts it in crisis.[11]

I have suggested that the matrix productive of experience is neither a metaphysical nor a transcendental structure—it is an arrangement of life whose form is police. The security of meaning and law, progress and reason, that is anchored in the endless gathering of property as plantation—this lies in the activity of policing that is simultaneously the voiding of play and relation and difference. It is not only that our interactions are corralled and proscribed into a specific mode of access to the world in which dependence on alterity is preemptively renounced. The seemingly "harmonious" nature of much social interaction should be understood to be an effect of the laminated sedimentation of crystallized policing. The impossible "world" of colonial modernity is barely cohesive.

This suggests that while we draw attention to the limitations of political projects and harm reduction, we should also draw attention to the obsession with absolute novelty that plagues structural reassurance as much as reformism. The structure of novelty is dependent on an impossibility that sutures temporality to a dialectical stutter between fatalism and stasis. Valorizing the "radically" new is thus born of a desire to both reify and deny the conditions through which the world itself requires continual founding and refounding.

In this sense, Fanonian invention should not be anticipated as rupture from without. Colonial modernity's processing of alterity renders otherness impossibly absolute, but difference is mundane and pervasive. This thought points toward the practical, psychic,

11. Marriott, *Lacan*, 138.

and social reliance of history's attempted suturing on the incessant policing of alterity. Fanon's understanding of invention as rupture in history, as Marriott suggests, is not therefore a rupture within an overcoded and calculable structure of time. Invention cannot merely be that which escapes the calculable, because history itself is everywhere fraught with crisis and rupture.

The previous chapter discussed how the endless perpetuation of emancipation is supposed to read as progress insofar as it indexes the movement across the boundary between slavery and freedom. However, as Binder considers, emancipation might also require the elimination of the boundary itself—so that both slavery and freedom are abolished.[12] Expanding through this, abolitionism may be conceived as the elimination of the boundaries and poles produced through a breach sewn into the world as police: that order and disorder, slave and master, colonizer and colonized, law and nature, may be eradicated alike.

Abolitionism therefore necessarily exceeds and divests from teleologies and dialectical resolution.[13] In line with the preceding discussion of Fanon, abolitionism, Jared Sexton suggests, could then "never finally be a politics of resurgence, recovery, or recuperation. It could only ever begin with degeneration, decline, or dissolution."[14] Not possible new worlds but rather the beyond, the impossible, abolitionism imagines the yet-to-come that is already present: the after-the-political that occurs also before.[15] The drive toward worlding through police cannot suture, cannot shut down

12. Binder, "Slavery," 2073.

13. Many of the ideas here were developed in conversation with Petero Kalulé; see, e.g., Petero Kalulé and James Trafford, "Unforming Police: The Impossibility of abolition," *Critical Legal Thinking,* December 1, 2020, https://criticallegalthinking.com/2020/12/01/unforming-police-the -impossibility-of-abolition/.

14. Jared Sexton, "The Vel of Slavery: Tracking the Figure of the Unsovereign," *Critical Sociology* 42, no. 4–5 (2016): 583–97.

15. Kara Keeling, "Looking for M—: Queer Temporality, Black Political Possibility and Poetry from the Future," *GLQ* 15, no. 4 (2009): 565.

the inventions of care that are necessarily always elsewhere—that cannot be delimited because they are there before, after, elsewhere than the violence of police and property. This alterity of futurity that cannot be fully sutured and bound under colonial modernity does not require that we accept the codes of history as unilinear and calculable. Rather, history is born of frenetic violence, but as such, it is fundamentally incapable of accessing or precluding invention.

Nothing less than the endless abolition of worlds—
abolitionism without end/s

Acknowledgments

With gratefulness beyond measure for our conversations and care, the food made and drinks shared, the voice-notes and cat videos, the play and encouragement—for love without finality, direction, or end . . . (especially Petals Kalulé + Melayna Lamb + Amy Etherington + Lynda Fitzwater + Mags + Zols + Cos)

(Continued from page iii)

Forerunners: Ideas First

Tia Trafford is reader in philosophy and design at the University for the Creative Arts. They are author of *The Empire at Home: Internal Colonies and the End of Britain.*